THE RISE OF LAW AND ECONOMICS

This is a history—though, intentionally, a brief history—of the rise of law and economics as a field of thought in the U.S. college and law school academy, though the field has expanded to Europe and South America and will expand further as other legal systems develop.

This book explains the origins of the field and the sources of its growth during its formative period. It describes the intellectual roots of the field, and the field's relationship to the understanding of the role of the legal system in directing the functioning of the economy. It describes the effect of the Great Depression and the expansion of governmental power on advancing the functional approach. The book then addresses the work of Aaron Director, during the late 1950s, on focusing economic analysis as a means of understanding the effects of the legal and regulatory system on the allocation of resources in the society. Then it turns to the subsequent intellectual founders of the field—Ronald Coase, Guido Calabresi, and Richard Posner—and attempts to explain the significance of their work. It also discusses the efforts of Robert Bork and Henry Manne toward the influence of law and economics on public policy. The book ends with the founding of the American Law and Economics Association in 1991.

This is an essential companion to law and economics texts for undergraduate law and economic students and, especially, a general supplement to first-year casebooks for law school students.

George L. Priest is the Edward J. Phelps Professor of Law and Economics at Yale Law School.

"As a witness to the rise of law and economics in the post-war United States, Professor Priest provides an elegantly written history of the big ideas that continue to inspire research and spark debate across established and emerging fields, from economics to public policy."

— *Marc D. Froese*, Professor of Political Science, Burman University

"This book reviews the growth and influence of the field of law and economics from World War II to 1991. It is a remarkable intellectual history, that carefully dissects the respective contributions made by the prime movers of the field, how their approaches differed, and how they influenced each other."

— *Stephen J. Spurr*, Professor of Economics, Wayne State University

THE RISE OF LAW AND ECONOMICS

An Intellectual History

George L. Priest

Routledge
Taylor & Francis Group
LONDON AND NEW YORK

First published 2020
by Routledge
2 Park Square, Milton Park, Abingdon, Oxon OX14 4RN

and by Routledge
52 Vanderbilt Avenue, New York, NY 10017

Routledge is an imprint of the Taylor & Francis Group, an informa business

British Library Cataloguing-in-Publication Data
A catalogue record for this book is available from the British Library

Library of Congress Cataloging-in-Publication Data
Names: Priest, George L., 1947- author.
Title: The rise of law and economics : an intellectual history / George L. Priest.
Description: Abingdon, Oxon ; New York, NY : Routledge, 2020. | Includes bibliographical references and index.
Identifiers: LCCN 2019054014 (print) | LCCN 2019054015 (ebook)
Subjects: LCSH: Law and economics–History. | Law and economics–Study and teaching–United States. | Law–Economic aspects–United States.
Classification: LCC K487.E3 P75 2020 (print) | LCC K487.E3 (ebook) | DDC 340/.11–dc23
LC record available at https://lccn.loc.gov/2019054014
LC ebook record available at https://lccn.loc.gov/2019054015

ISBN: 978-0-367-33937-1 (hbk)
ISBN: 978-0-367-33938-8 (pbk)
ISBN: 978-0-429-32294-5 (ebk)

Typeset in Bembo
by Swales & Willis, Exeter, Devon, UK

For T, C, N, and J.
With deepest love.

CONTENTS

FIGURES

ACKNOWLEDGEMENTS

My relation to law and economics

Many of the central figures of modern law and economics whose work I discuss in this book were teachers of mine, and friends. This book, however, is not a memoir. I have reread all of the writings I discuss in the light of my many subsequent decades of work in the field. I have tried to present a faithful explication of the great accomplishments of these scholars that have led to the enormous success of law and economics.

My immersion in law and economics began in 1970 as a student at the University of Chicago Law School. At that time, my principal academic interest was legal history. But I was startled in one legal history class when a graduate participant, listening to the class's discussion of the effects of some legal rule, interjected that Ronald Coase—a professor at the Law School—had shown that such an analysis was superficial and that the case ruling being discussed would have no effect.

This point shocked me. The participant was highly intelligent, so I took the claim seriously. Following this, I read Coase's seminal article "The Problem of Social Cost" very carefully; it took me two weeks to complete and to try to understand it (even after later rereadings, it remains a dense article). Thereafter, I took every course that Ronald Coase taught, and became something of a close student of Coase. Over some period, Coase would invite his faculty protégé John Peterman and me to lunch twice a week.

I also took every class of Richard Posner, who later hired me as a research assistant to work on a paper that Coase had urged him to write. I also took classes from other members of the law and economics faculty at Chicago such as Edmund Kitch and John Peterman. Interested in becoming an academic, I also attended George Stigler's Industrial Organization Workshop, among whose participants were Gary Becker and Sam Peltzman, among others.

I entered academia after law school. Two years later, Ronald Coase invited me to become a research fellow in his Law and Economics program at Chicago. I served there from 1975 to 1977. There I met and learned from other central law and economics scholars: William Landes and Kenneth Dam, in particular. I also got to know Gary Becker more closely, often attending his classes, and, over later years, became a good friend of Becker. During my time there, Ed Kitch arranged for me to be invited to a Henry Manne Conference, one of many that I attended thereafter. Henry also became a good friend.

As an academic, I moved to UCLA in 1979. There I met and became close friends with Harold Demsetz—an iconic law and economics scholar—Armen Alchian, and Ben Klein, all in the economics department, among many others.

I moved to Yale Law School in 1980. The leading law and economics figure at Yale, Guido Calabresi, was on leave for the year. Anticipating his return, I carefully read his seminal book, *The Costs of Accidents*, though it took me several weeks to fully complete it. Guido returned the next year, and has been a colleague and friend since.

Robert Bork was on the faculty at the time I visited there, but I had no interaction with him. After he had left the Law School faculty, I recognized him on a flight to Chicago, though we sat in different air fare classes. Bob, however, generously offered me a ride from the airport and we had a good talk. We later interacted frequently, especially, many years later, around the Microsoft case, over which we had several public debates, in which my part consisted of quoting passages from Bork's book *The Antitrust Paradox* that, to my reading, contested Bork's then-criticism of Microsoft. Bork and I became good friends.

Later, I would become involved in the founding of the American Law and Economics Association.

I gratefully acknowledge the lessons of these great teachers even though I am certain that those who have died may not have agreed, and those living will not entirely agree, with my analysis.

This book builds on earlier work. In 1982—37 years ago—I wrote an early version of this history for a symposium to be published in the *Journal of Legal Education* (AALS and Emory 1983). I declined to publish that article, however (much to the ire of the symposium editor, Roger Cramton). My then-new colleague, Guido Calabresi, complained that the article was a "Chicago" history—which it was—and that I should not publish my (modest) criticisms of Calabresi's work until I had read the writings of Fleming James. Thus, I declined publication in the symposium. I then read Fleming James and later published an article addressing, among other matters, James' ideas and work (Priest 1985). Nevertheless, my then-colleague Judith Jarvis Thompson and her Harvard colleague John Rawls urged me to turn the article into a book, which I have not done until now, though with many changes.

Guido was right, however. Reading James led me to a new appreciation of Guido's work, which a recent rereading of *The Costs of Accidents* and other Calabresi articles and books has only magnified. The 1981 article, however, had been earlier published without serious change (Priest 2005). This book presents a revised interpretation of Calabresi's achievements.

I have also written about the late Aaron Director (Priest 2010), my late teacher Ronald Coase (Priest 2014a), my late colleague, Robert Bork (Priest 2008; 2014b), and of the late Henry Manne (Priest 1999).

This book draws from those earlier pieces, but hopefully extends the analysis of each of them.

I am grateful for comments on earlier chapters of this book, especially from Guido Calabresi, but also from Claire Priest (who suggested the photos), Owen Fiss, Bill Eskridge, Justin Driver, participants at a faculty workshop at Yale Law School and at the American Law and Economics Association Meetings in 2018, and from two anonymous reviewers. I am also grateful to Alison MacKeen for editorial advice.

I am deeply grateful to Karen Crocco, who has faithfully input seemingly endless changes to this manuscript.

1

INTRODUCTION

Law and economics can be identified today as the dominant academic discipline in understanding the rule of law in the United States and, increasingly, around the world. It informs—directs—obvious economic areas such as antitrust, regulation, and corporate organization but also all other areas of law: torts, contracts, property, and environmental law, among many others.

Law and economics concepts also inform vast areas of governmental activity. Of course, there is inevitably an economic component to direct governmental regulation of industry, but the content of regulation has been dramatically changed as law and economics scholarship has progressed, both refining operative regulatory tools and eliminating vast areas of governmental regulation entirely. Moreover, the direct regulation of manufacturing in specific industries—such as of safety features in automobiles, of occupational health and safety in the workplace, of environmental regulation, and of health care, as examples—is now dominated by concepts deriving from law and economics.

This book attempts to explain the origins of the field and the sources of its growth during its formative period. It describes the intellectual origins of the field, and the field's relationship to the understanding of the role of the legal system in directing the functioning of the economy. It discusses the history of the field from its earliest origins in the 1940s and 1950s (and earlier) to 1991, at the founding of the American Law and Economics Association.

There are many origins, though the most important of them, in terms of purely intellectual achievement and direction, derived from academic work completed or inspired by scholars at the University of Chicago Law School and at Yale Law School.

The successes of these purely academic endeavors followed the increasing adoption over the twentieth century of a functional approach to thinking about the role of law in a society. The shift in the conception of the role of the legal system as moving beyond merely a definition of rights—such as the right to own personal property and the right to freely enter contracts—to thinking about the legal system more functionally—what are and what should be the functional effects of legal rules regarding property and contracts—began at the end of the nineteenth century and has continued progressively since then.

At the end of the nineteenth century, the predominant view of the law was that it consisted of a set of constant, immutable rules, explicated in Harvard Law School's Dean Christopher Langdell's casebooks and, similarly, enforced by the Supreme Court to protect the right to own private property and an individual's liberty of contract. The legal system had been employed—though sparingly—toward the regulation of some industries since the late nineteenth century—chiefly some railroads and some public utilities (Kahn 1970–71; McCraw 1984)—to achieve the functions of prohibiting price-fixing and maintaining competition, though the economic analysis in designing this regulation was quite crude. The functional conception of law, however, was accelerated by the Depression of the 1930s with the extraordinary disruption of the society that resulted. From that experience, a consensus emerged involving a greatly enhanced role of government generally, including a more aggressive conception of the possible role of legal rules and regulations, aimed toward enhancing the welfare of the society.

Given the acceptance of a functional view of the role of law, law and economics emerged as the most powerful and most defensible method for implementing that approach and so has affected both government policy and the work of the academy.

The greatest successes in the field of law and economics generated from Chicago: from the work of Aaron Director, who founded the *Journal of Law & Economics*; from the achievements, as his successor as Editor of that *Journal*, of Ronald H. Coase; from the work of Richard A. Posner, and from many others.

The work that Director and Coase encouraged and supported chiefly addressed issues of industrial organization, including antitrust law and regulation in the United States. As shall be shown, that work probably demonstrates the greatest direct influence of modern law and economics ideas on current law.

As part of his project studying regulation, Director asked Coase, who was not then at Chicago, but who had written earlier on British broadcasting, to study the U.S. Federal Communications Commission. In this study, Coase developed startling economic insights later, and most prominently, presented in his exceptional article "The Problem of Social Cost," published in 1960, which revolutionized the analysis of the function of common-law rules by extending the importance of economic analysis far beyond antitrust and regulation to all of law. Coase showed that the assignment of liability of a legal rule will have no effect on the allocation of resources, given markets to overcome it, except for the existence of transaction costs which constrain market exchange.

This demonstration shocked the legal community, though it took some time because the *Journal of Law & Economics* was then not a central journal in the law school world. The standard view, in contrast, was that the law and legal rules or liability findings affected activity in the society: for example, a rule that made a party who had dammed or flooded a river liable for resulting damages to a downstream property owner would cause that activity to end. Coase's point, from an economic standpoint, was that that simple conclusion was indeterminate, and depended on the relative value of the competing upstream and downstream resources and the magnitude of transaction costs, a matter never considered in the standard view. Coase's paper constituted a revolution in legal analysis brought about by the application of economics.

Roughly a decade later, in the early 1970s, Richard A. Posner, ingeniously developed a theory that all common-law rules were efficient in the sense of optimizing the costs and benefits generated by the rules on social behavior. Posner's radical idea, and the extraordinary support that he and his accomplished colleague William M. Landes provided to support that theory, purporting to show the efficiency of *all* common-law rules, sub-area by sub-area, equally shocked the legal academy. Because Posner's application extended to all of law, it forced virtually all legal scholars to define themselves for or against this version of law and economics. Coase's initial shock, though it took time for it to be understood, and Posner's later work, brought law and economics to the forefront of legal academic debates.

The greatest success of the Yale approach was the work on accident law of my colleague Guido Calabresi. Calabresi, who preceded Posner, analyzed tort law from an economic perspective beginning in "Some Thoughts on Risk Distribution and the Law of Torts," an important article published in 1961, essentially explaining tort law's deterrent functions as well as arguing that the rules of the law had risk and wealth distributional effects, insisting upon the importance of these distributional effects to the analysis of otherwise purely deterrent issues (Calabresi 1961). Calabresi's formulation, generalized in his important 1970 book *The Costs of Accidents*, definitively established the economic basis of the functional analysis of law. Posner, following Calabresi, adopted a similar economic framework, but differed by disclaiming any role for distributional concerns in his efficiency analysis.

In the early years, Calabresi and Posner debated the importance of wealth distributional concerns in thinking about the law. The combat between Calabresi and Posner energized attention to the field. But, after these initial works, Calabresi directed his research to higher levels of theory (writing many important books and papers on topics less related to law and economics); Posner's work seemed empirical—most papers were based on exhaustive studies of all cases dealing with a particular subject—and the publication of many seemingly empirical papers by Posner and by Posner and Landes made the debate difficult for the Calabresians.

At the same time, and significantly contributing to the advance of the field, were important efforts by Henry Manne, who can be described as an evangelical in pursuit of the transcendence of law and economics. Manne himself was a considerable law and economics scholar, trained at Chicago (though he also had a Yale graduate law degree, which he seldom acknowledged). Manne developed the idea of the market for corporate control (now universally accepted) and raised telling theoretical criticisms of restrictions on corporate insider trading (which remain ahead of their time). These two ideas have become deeply significant to the understanding and legal control of corporate behavior.

Perhaps Manne's greatest achievement, however, was his promotion of law and economics as a discipline: first, through organizing training sessions in economics for non-acquainted legal academics and some attorneys to learn about economic analysis, and organizing similar sessions for economists to learn about the law; second, through organizing an extraordinary series of conferences for federal judges to teach basic economic principles; and third, through organizing conferences that enlisted academics to discuss current major issues in law and economics.

As shall be explained, the advance of law and economics has transformed the way that legal issues are described in all areas of law and, as a consequence, how these issues are resolved. It has had its most important tangible success to date in the field of regulation and antitrust law. With respect to industry regulation, scholarship in law and economics can be said to have vastly improved the effects of regulatory methods but, also, to have generated the deregulation movement, in which many federal regulatory agencies have had their authority limited or were eliminated altogether. This scholarship has substantially slowed subsequent ambitions to extend regulation. In the field of antitrust law, since the mid-1970s, the U.S. Supreme Court has radically revised its approach to antitrust analysis, essentially adopting the Aaron Director Chicago School approach. This change in Supreme Court doctrine was importantly influenced by my late colleague Robert H. Bork, who had first served as a Research Associate under Aaron Director, though later, and importantly, as Solicitor General, and by Richard A. Posner, who had also learned from Director.

These various intellectual achievements all contributed toward the adoption of the functional approach to law, with economic analysis emerging as the primary instrument in explicating that functional approach. Because of its dominance as theory, its empirical dominance toward understanding the effects of law in comparison to any other approach, and, to a much lesser extent, to the belief of many of its practitioners that market decisions about the allocation of resources are superior to government decisions, law and economics has become the predominant intellectual approach both to understanding the content of the law and to the direction of future law, both in government and in the academy.

The rise of law and economics has been spectacular. Solely as an indication, in 1960 at the time of Calabresi's "Some Thoughts on Risk Distribution" and Coase's "The Problem of Social Cost," Harvard Law School had no full-time economists on its faculty and one what I would call a lawyer-economist.[1] The University of Chicago Law School had one economist[2] and no lawyer-economists. Stanford Law School had no economists but one lawyer-economist.[3] Yale had one economist and one lawyer-economist.[4]

Three decades later, at the founding of the American Law & Economics Association in 1991, Harvard had on its full-time faculty three full-time economists[5] and three lawyer-economists.[6] Chicago had two full-time economists[7] and seven lawyer-economists.[8] Stanford had three economists[9] and four lawyer-economists,[10] and Yale had three economists[11] and six lawyer-economists.[12]

Today, as I write in 2019, Harvard has six full-time Ph.D economists[13] and eight lawyer-economists,[14] Chicago has two Ph.D economists[15] and eleven lawyer-economists,[16] Stanford has four Ph.D economists[17] and eight lawyer-economists,[18] and Yale has seven Ph.D economists[19] and eight lawyer-economists.[20] The American Law and Economics Association, again formed in 1991, has 656 members.

1 By this, I mean a lawyer whose chief intellectual methodology is economic analysis: at Harvard, Donald Turner, who had a Ph.D in economics but only wrote on legal issues.
2 Director, who did not have a Ph.D.
3 Baxter.
4 Ward S. Bowman, Jr,. who did not have a Ph.D but was a full-time economist, and Guido Calabresi.
5 Shavell, Bebchuck, and Kaplow.
6 Areeda, Jackson, and Kraakman.
7 Coase, who did not have a Ph.D, and Landes.
8 Baird, Dam, Epstein, Fischel, Macey, Miller, and Picker.
9 Campbell, Polinsky, and Strnad.
10 Baxter, Gilson, Grundfest, and Scott.
11 Hansmann, Klevorick, and Rose-Ackerman.
12 Calabresi, Ellickson, G. Priest, Romano, Schwartz, and Winter.
13 Bar-Gill, Bebchuck, Elhauge, Kaplow, Shavell, and Spier.
14 Coates, Fried, Hay, Jackson, Kraakman, Ramseyer, Sitkoff, and Smith.
15 Ben-Shahar, and Landes (retired, but still listed on the faculty).
16 Baird, Bernstein, Dam (retired), Fennell, Fischel (retired), Hemel, Levmore, Picker, E. Posner, Strahilovitz, and Weisbach.
17 Donohue, Polinsky, Strnad, and Sykes.
18 Bankman, Craswell (retired), Daines, Grundfest, Kessler, Lemly, Scott (retired), and Triantis.
19 Ayres, Hansmann, Jolls, Klevorick, Liskow, Listokin, and Rose-Ackerman.
20 Calabresi, Ellickson, Macey, Morley, C. Priest, G. Priest, Romano, and Schwartz. Other major law schools had similar histories. At Michigan, for example, in 1960, no economics Ph.Ds and two lawyer-economists (Kauper and Oppenheim, both teaching antitrust); in 2019, one Ph.D economist (Fox) and three lawyer-economists (Crane, Kauper, and Logue). At NYU, in 1960, no Ph.Ds and one lawyer-economist (Schwartz, teaching antitrust); in 2019, three Ph.Ds (Ferejohn, Kahan, and Kornhauser) and thirteen lawyer-economists (Adler, Arlen, Davis, First, Fox, Geistfeld, Hemphill, Mariotta-Wagler, Miller, Revesz, Rock, Sharkey, and Shaviro). At Penn, in 1960, no Ph.Ds and two lawyer-economists (Henkin and Schwartz, both teaching antitrust); in 2019, two Ph.Ds (Chang and Santirico) and nine lawyer-economists (Baker, Fisch, Gelbach, Hovenkamp, Mundheim, Parchamovsky, Wax, Yoo, and Wachter).

There has also occurred a broad expansion of law and economics study and teaching abroad. In addition to the American Law and Economics Association, there exists today the European Association of Law and Economics, the Latin American and Iberian Law and Economics Association, the Australian Law and Economics Association, the Canadian Law and Economics Association, the Law and Economics Association of New Zealand, the Midwestern Law and Economics Association, the Brazilian Association of Law and Economics, the Asian Law & Economics Association, the Israeli Law and Economics Association, the German Law and Economics Association, the Italian Society of Law and Economics, the Spanish Association of Law and Economics, the Greek Association of Law and Economics, and the Polish Association of Law & Economics.

This book will describe the rise of law and economics during its formative period. It attempts to explain the early beginnings as the legal system began to develop a functional approach to law. It describes the effect of the Great Depression and the expansion of governmental power on advancing the functional approach. It then addresses the work of Aaron Director, during the late 1950s, on focusing economic analysis as a means of understanding the effects of the legal and regulatory system on the allocation of resources in the society.

The book then turns to the subsequent intellectual founders of the field—Ronald Coase, Guido Calabresi, and Richard Posner—and attempts to explain the significance of their work. The book also discusses the efforts of Robert Bork and Henry Manne toward the influence of law and economics on public policy. The book ends with the founding of the American Law and Economics Association in 1991.

There have been many developments in the field since then that are not discussed, such as the growth of the fields of public choice, game theory, experimental law and economics, and behavioral law and economics. These developments and many other innovative ideas in law and economics are not unimportant, but they do not impact the understanding of the formative period of the field.

2

THE EARLY DEVELOPMENT OF THE FUNCTIONAL APPROACH TO LAW

Though there were surely earlier precursors, the beginning most directly related to the modern use of the law functionally, to achieve identifiable economic effects, was the adoption of regulatory systems by many states. Massachusetts imposed regulation on railroads in 1871. State regulation was resisted by industry, but was held to be allowed by the U.S. Constitution in 1877, in a case involving the regulation of grain elevators (*Munn* 1877). The economic effect of these early regulatory efforts is not clear. They were designed to prohibit the most extreme forms of price fixing or revenue pooling, but their ultimate economic influence on societal welfare remains largely unmeasured. The effect of these new ambitions for state government, implemented through the law, on the consideration of private law issues has also not been studied.

As firms in a great many American industries began to consolidate after the Civil War, advanced attention was given to means of controlling industrial behavior. Many states enacted anti-trust laws in the 1880s.[1] The U.S. Congress created the first agency to regulate an industry in 1887: the Interstate Commerce Commission, which was assigned the duty of regulating railroads. The principal provisions of the Interstate Commerce Act were to prohibit railroad pooling of revenues (which, obviously, was a method to share the resources from fixed prices); to regulate railroad tariffs, though not to directly set rates, but in particular to prevent railroads from granting rebates to shippers; and to eliminate differential rates, as between long- and short-haul transport.

1 Trusts were a legal technique of allowing firms to coordinate interstate commerce, since state incorporation grants at the time almost uniformly prohibited corporations within a state from ownership of shares of out-of-state corporations. The creation of a trust, with corporations ceding their shares in return for trust certificates, where the shares would be administered by trustees, allowed interstate control. The trust form, of course, was later challenged.

There was some economic content to these ambitions, but only some. The prohibition of pooling makes economic sense. The Commission's prohibition of rebates on tariffs had political importance, but was of questionable economic value. Shipping rebates are the equivalent of price reductions to the benefit of shippers and ultimately, given competition, to the benefit of consumers. Rebates do not benefit railroads; they reduce revenues. The prohibition of rebates protected the railroads from competition over rebates with other railroads.

It is apparent, however, that the prohibition of railroad rebates also served to protect small shippers versus large. Rebates on announced railroad tariffs were obtained by large shippers that could induce a railroad to grant a rebate on charges for large shipments with the threat of taking its more substantial trade to another railroad (Priest 2012). This reflects monopsony power of the large shipper. Small shippers possessed no equivalent economic power. Thus, the prohibition of rebates served a distributional purpose in favor of small shippers. How effective the prohibition was has not been conclusively determined.

The long-haul/short-haul prohibition was of the same nature: curtailing the railroad practice of charging higher rates for short-haul transport, where there was less railroad competition, than for long-haul transport, where competition was greater. This prohibition had nothing to do with railroad economics, or economics in general where prices are lower in more competitive environments, but served to benefit communities and shippers and consumers within those communities with no or little railroad competition.

Other state intervention in the economy also served chiefly political, rather than economic, ends. Among the most dramatic was the circumvention of the common law dealing with workplace accidents by the enactment of workers' compensation programs. These programs, enacted in the first decades of the century, represented the most radical reform of tort law of the preceding three hundred years. During the years that followed, a principal effort of tort scholars was to reconcile the common law of tort that remained (or remained to be reformed) with the theories that justified workers' compensation. Although in the legislatures the statutes were justified pragmatically—as a worker-management compromise of automatic recovery for lower dollar amounts paid for injuries (*Ives* 1911)—in the journals, the justifications were more rigorous and more principled. It became widely accepted that losses from injuries to workers represented a "cost" of enterprise and that the compensation statutes served to internalize these costs to the responsible corporate decision makers (J. Smith 1914a, 1914b; Thayer 1916). It also became accepted that businesses could bear these costs more adequately than could injured workers because businesses could internalize them by passing them along to consumers in the prices of their products (Thayer 1916; Cohen 1916). This is basically an economic idea, though a simple economic idea. The central question for contemporary tort scholarship was how far to extend the internalization concept and how the concept related to then-prevailing standards of tort law.

Putting aside Langdell's views that the principles of private law were determinable and fixed, the dominant theoretical approach of the period—moving toward a functional approach—was the benefit theory of Francis Bohlen, who was later chosen Reporter of the first Restatement of Torts.[2] Bohlen explained the rules of tort law as consistent with the principle that a "duty" in tort law, an affirmative obligation to secure the safety of others,[3] is imposed only on those who have voluntarily assumed a position or relation from which they benefit from actions of the victim that put the victim at risk.[4] Bohlen's best evidence was the distinction in tort law among a landowner's obligations to invitees, licensees, and trespassers, from whose activities, respectively, a landowner always, sometimes, and never benefits.[5] Bohlen's theory, however, was also attractive because of the unifying framework it established for understanding all of civil law, as we will see, an important feature of the modern success of law and economics. Bohlen explained the benefit requirement of tort law as the exact counterpart of the consideration requirement of contract law that provided that contracts could only be enforced if some consideration—benefit—passed between the parties to the contract.[6]

Bohlen was a leading advocate of workers' compensation. He had studied English and European compensation systems, had drafted the statute enacted in Pennsylvania, and later served as counsel for the Pennsylvania Workmen's Compensation Board.[7] Some of Bohlen's writings describe workers' compensation statutes as exceptions to the common law, responsive to humanitarian concerns about the welfare of injured workers and their families (Bohlen 1912 at 401, 517). In other passages, however, Bohlen reconciles the statutes with the benefit theory. A workers' compensation system is consistent with the benefit theory if one regards the crucial transaction in the employer–employee–customer relationship to be the exchange between the employer and the customer. According to Bohlen, the worker, like machinery or raw materials, constitutes only an element of, an input into, the process leading to the mutually beneficial exchange between the business entity and the customer. Thus, as between the employer and the worker in the industrial injury context, the employer receives *all* the benefit.[8] A compensation system establishing automatic recovery for workers' injuries follows directly. Bohlen made clear, however, that for all other tortious relationships, the legal implication of the benefit theory is the negligence

2 Francis H. Bohlen 1905 at 209, 273, 337.

3 Bohlen viewed the rules of intentional torts as requiring no explanation.

4 Bohlen 1905, at 273.

5 *Id.* at 220–235.

6 *Id.* at 218–219.

7 See Eldredge 1943 at 390.

8 *Id.* This proposition, however, was questioned in J. Smith 1914a, at 252–253; and in Mechem 1910 at 241–242.

standard with the contributory negligence and assumption of risk defenses (Bohlen 1905a, 1905b).

From my readings, Bohlen's approach was regarded as—and was—the most developed and sophisticated theory of tort law of the time. Bohlen's benefit theory, however, was only one of a number of contemporary justifications of negligence as the central standard of tort law. Jeremiah Smith trumpeted the modernity of the negligence standard in contrast to principles of absolute liability thought appropriate in the Middle Ages (Smith 1914a, at 237–241). Terry espoused the negligence standard because it provided a method to balance the multitude or risk and value questions relevant in tort cases (Terry 1915).[9] Thayer argued that there was no justification whatsoever for a *Rylands v. Fletcher* standard of liability without fault that failed to take the circumstances of the event into account (Thayer 1916). Some years later, Fowler Harper demonstrated that an absolute liability standard was extremely difficult to define and that there were no clear examples of such a standard at common law (Harper 1932).

Later in the period, toward the end of Bohlen's career, one small group of scholars struggled to extend the principle of workers' compensation to the area of automobile accidents. In 1932, the Columbia Automobile Accident Project, led by Charles E. Clark, proposed the adoption of a system of liability of automobile owners to injured parties without regard to the fault of owners, drivers, or victims. The proposal provided for the recovery of damages equal to those awarded under the local workers' compensation system drawn from a fund to be supported by compulsory insurance (Committee 1932). The principal motivation of the committee was humanitarian; its report documented at length how tort law inadequately compensated auto victims, particularly the poor.[10] The committee also justified its proposal in Bohlen's terms: automobile owners were the chief beneficiaries of driving and compulsory insurance would internalize the costs of driving to them.[11]

These scholars had adopted what may be regarded as an economic idea. By forcing parties that cause harm to pay the costs of that harm—here personal injury damages—those costs are "internalized" to the harm-causer, compelling it to take those costs into account in its determination of how it operates in society. At this point in the development of the idea, the internalization point may be grounded in morals, rather than in economics—it is *just* to have the harm-causing party pay for the losses—though it has an economic base as well. It represents a movement, nevertheless, toward conceiving of the law in functional terms. As the internalization idea becomes more precise, it becomes an economic idea.

9 In recent years, Landes and Posner have claimed Terry's article as a precursor to their efficiency theory of the law, discussed in Ch. 7, *infra*. The article instead is a jumbled and poorly organized discussion of rules for assigning negligence according to five separate factors, only some of which are relevant to the wealth-maximization hypothesis of Landes and Posner.

10 Committee 1932 at 53–71, 91–95, 202–206, 220–235.

11 *Id.* at 136–136.

The attention to a functional approach to law was certainly accelerated by the Depression, which seriously upset the idea—the belief—that the current organization of the society, including its laws, was working effectively. The constitutional regime in place prior to the Depression was called the "substantive Due Process" school because the U.S. Supreme Court employed the constitutional guaranty of legal due process to consistently invoke substantive principles of the right to own private property and the liberty of private contract, to reject broader efforts to enact social legislation. The Depression was interpreted by many to show that that set of ideas was dysfunctional, leading to the need for massive changes in social policy.

The Realists, a group of scholars who opposed the Supreme Court's view of the organization of society, attempted to provide an alternative approach to the law. The Realists tried to show, often through quite weak empirical studies, that the law in fact did not correspond to the law defined by principles of right to property and freedom of contract as conceived by the Supreme Court. The Realist effort, from an academic standpoint, failed because the Realists had no alternative theory of social organization.

The Realists, however, did influence the rise of law and economics, although only indirectly. There were no economists among the Realists,[12] and no economic content to Realist scholarship. Nevertheless, the Realists succeeded in convincing the academic world of the possibility that social science could explain the deeper foundations of the law. The Realist research program itself was a failure. The empirical work—principally atheoretical—showed nothing and led to little reform. The interest of the Realists in an empirical understanding of the legal system was limited, especially after many Realists became New Deal advocates and some, New Deal officials. Thus, with few exceptions, the empirical method was abandoned with the coming of the New Deal. The Realist challenge to legal scholarship, however, planted in the consciousness of legal academics the dream that social science could explain the legal system.

12 Walton Hamilton was trained as an economist, but he taught standard law courses at Yale, and his writings do not reflect an economic approach. His work at the Temporary National Economic Committee postdated the Realist movement.

3

THE PROBLEMS OF THE DEPRESSION AND THE BROADER ACCEPTANCE OF THE FUNCTIONAL APPROACH TO LAW

The cataclysm of the Great Depression led to vast changes in social policy. The principal effects of the Depression were the huge increase in unemployment, the dramatic fall in wages, and the steep drop in the price level. In the U.S, as in many western European countries, governments used these economic phenomena to expand their authority to regulate and direct business enterprise as well as to redistribute resources among the citizens, somewhat, but not entirely, to the lower-income.

A centerpiece of New Deal legislation in the United States was the National Industrial Recovery Act (NIRA), which sought to implement policies to increase wages and increase prices, believing that these policies would improve the welfare of workers and business at the same time.[1] To achieve these ambitions, the federal government created the National Recovery Administration, empowered to organize "Councils" for every U.S. industry, comprising representatives from all major companies within each industry along with representatives of labor. These Councils were authorized to promulgate "Codes of Fair Competition," setting wages for workers in each industry—at a higher level than previously prevailing wages—and fixing higher prices for each industry's product sales. These policies basically set cartel prices both for labor and industry.

Before legal challenges, 634 Councils were established, each for a separate U.S. industry. The individual Councils met, defined their respective Code of Fair Competition setting prices and wages, and began implementation. After only a short period, however, the U.S. Supreme Court held the NIRA

1 There was a political dimension to these reforms as well, not only to seek the support of the benefited groups, but larger, because Roosevelt wanted policies that increased wages in contrast to Stalin's policies during the period that reduced wages.

unconstitutional as an improper delegation of Congressional powers (*A. L. A. Schechter* 1935). The actual economic effect of the Councils and of the NIRA has not been accurately measured.

Today, the law and economics community views these early New Deal policies not only as economically naïve, but as directly harmful to economic welfare. Surely, important phenomena of the Great Depression were a fall in the price level, a fall in wages, and dramatic increases in unemployment. The events are now understood as deriving, initially, from the bursting of a stock market bubble, but then exacerbated by deeply mistaken monetary policies of the Federal Reserve which sought to increase U.S. economic strength by raising interest rates in order to attract foreign gold to the United States, then still on the gold standard. In this context, the policies of the NIRA, such as artificially raising wages, would increase, not decrease, unemployment (though affected workers would benefit). Similarly, raising industrial prices would diminish the resources available to the citizenry. Thus, the NIRA and its policies, to the extent that they were implemented, extended, rather than relieved, the economic problems of the Depression.

Following the Supreme Court's invalidation of the NIRA and other early New Deal legislation, political forces compelled the Supreme Court to reverse its Due Process constitutional approach and to authorize under the Constitution vast areas of federal control over the economy. The law and legal regulations took on a new purpose, consistent with this new view of the role of government. But, at a later period, President Roosevelt and the Congress did not reenact the cartel policies of the NIRA. Instead, in what is called the Second New Deal, Roosevelt embraced a policy of improving the economy through the antitrust laws: by stimulating industrial competition. Roosevelt appointed Thurman Arnold as chief of the Justice Department's Antitrust Division.

Arnold was then a Yale Law School professor, writing popular books about the economy and industrial practices (Arnold 1937, 1940). He had no economic theory to guide his administration and, to my view, no economic knowledge. (He had been the Mayor of Laramie, Wyoming before entering academia.) Arnold did believe, however, in active antitrust prosecution by the government: the Justice Department filed more antitrust complaints under his tenure than in the forty-seven years from the enactment of the Sherman Act that had preceded his appointment.

His division brought many important lawsuits: some against the continuation of the industry cartel practices encouraged or created by the NIRA (*Socony* 1940); others that obtained important procedural advantages for government antitrust prosecutions (*Interstate Circuit* 1939). But, in retrospect, though Arnold's division sometimes relied on economic arguments—though typically simple economic arguments, such as the benefits of prohibiting price fixing—one cannot identify a coherent view, other than more antitrust prosecution is better than less, though coherency may be a standard too high for an official, such as Arnold, in a government agency. Arnold, however, surely invigorated the view that antitrust law should be a dominant element in the control of industrial enterprise. As shall be discussed, the later efforts of Aaron Director, leading to the development of modern law and economics, would respond to the increased importance of antitrust laws.

As the government began to use law and legal institutions to promote social values, the conception of the role of private law also underwent change, finally developing what I have called the functional approach: to define the law with an eye to the functional—most often economic—effects that it served. As discussed, the beginnings of the acceptance of the functional approach to law were reflected in the adoption of workers' compensation statutes by most states and the effort of the Columbia Automobile Accident Project, led by Charles E. Clark of Yale Law School, to adopt a similar compensation system for victims of auto accidents.

In the years shortly after, these efforts would accelerate as exemplified in the work of Fleming James, a Yale Law professor, who strove to apply and expand these compensation system ideas, and in the accelerating coordination of compensation plans to replace the common law of torts. James was surely not an economist, but his analysis and proposals had a simple economic base that he promoted with rudimentary empirical studies of an economic nature. They contributed substantially toward the adoption of the functional approach to law. Later, his ideas would be generalized and put into a purely economic framework by his protégé Guido Calabresi, who, along with Chicago's Coase and Posner, is one of the giants of modern law and economics. Calabresi's subsequent achievements (discussed in Chapter 6) can be better appreciated with a review of James' earlier work.

Fleming James entered law teaching in the mid-1930s, just as the country was recovering from the Depression, and within his first few years published proposals for the reform of the tort system that set forth the basic ideas of his career. After World War II, he resumed his scholarly program, and he became the dominant tort scholar of the 1940s and 1950s in terms of the volume, scope, and influence of his ideas. James' influence, however, was not immediate, and it cannot be attributed to the novelty or persuasiveness of his theories. James' work built on propositions well established at the turn of the century. Instead, James' influence, in my view, derived from his radical single-mindedness. From his earliest articles, James promoted one principle—risk distribution—above all others. Every other consideration that might be thought relevant to the resolution of a tort dispute, James ruthlessly devalued or ignored. This had an important effect on focusing the law to functional ends. Most importantly, he devised a program of research that, over time, came to exert a cumulative influence on tort law thinking that made risk distribution central to the understanding of tort law by the mid-1960s.

The single idea on which all of James' tort scholarship was built was the role of personal injury damage judgments as a form of "social insurance" (James 1938, 1941). James saw accidents as inevitable consequences of productive activity, and he conceived the principal function of tort law to be not the resolution of disputes, rule definition, or the expression of moral values, but compensation of the injured. The influence of the Depression was surely substantial here. James was greatly concerned about the consequences of serious personal injury on the lives of victims, most particularly the poor. And the problem he addressed was how to repair the lives of those victims to whom he referred in article after article as "helpless individuals" (James 1936), the "poor and weak" (James 1941), and those who can ill afford or are unable to bear the accident loss (James 1938; 1939 at 716). James believed that the direct answer to the problem was to shift losses from these plaintiffs to defendants able to spread them broadly over society by insuring or, if the defendants were manufacturers or service providers, by adding some small increment to the prices of their products, serving as a form of insurance (James 1939 at 212). James' understanding of insurance was naïve and consisted basically of the point that it is always better to divide a loss among a hundred individuals than to put it on any one. Loss distribution reduced the risk and uncertainty that would otherwise inhibit desirable activities by substituting a small calculable cost for the risk of a loss ruinous to a single individual (James 1939 at 1156). There is, however, some economic content to this idea.

These concerns led James to concentrate his tort law research on methods of improving the delivery of compensation to injured victims in ways that served to spread losses over society as a whole. "So my major proposition," James declared,

> is simply this: An existing rule of law which has some tendency to effect loss distribution over a large segment of society ought not to give way to a rule which will bring about a less effective distribution unless there is a very good reason for it.[2]

Put more concretely, James criticized any aspect of the tort system that reduced the likelihood of plaintiff recovery, since defendants more frequently than plaintiffs were enterprises well positioned to distribute risks (James 1939 at 208–210).

The focus on risk distribution led James to be severely critical of the fault system in its entirety (James 1941 at 1156). James objected both to the negligence requirement that denied recovery to plaintiffs unable to establish the defendant's fault and to the contributory negligence defense that denied recovery to plaintiffs who themselves had exhibited fault. According to James, the fault system derived from archaic notions of behavior (James 1938 at 709–714). In the modern world, "in the field of accidental injury, fault in the sense of clear

2 James 1939. I have suppressed James' emphasis of the entire passage. This is a conscious allusion to and reversal of Holmes' famous dictum in *The Common Law* (1881): "[the law's] cumbrous and expensive machinery ought not to be set in motion unless some clear benefit is to be derived ..." Holmes at 96.

moral delinquency is rare" (James 1941 at 1157). Physiological and psychological shortcomings "which a psychologist might regard as the inevitable outcome of heredity and environment" (James 1938 at 214) were much more likely to be involved. James did not believe that the prospect of damage liability would perceptibly deter accident-causing behavior, a conclusion questionable in my mind but basically economic (James 1936 at 161). James thought that accident prevention was more likely to be increased if large enterprises, such as insurance companies, promoted safety instruction and accident awareness programs.[3]

James hoped to replace the fault system with a comprehensive social insurance plan such as workers' compensation (James 1941 at 1156), although in his early writings he entertained the possibility of a compulsory private insurance regime (James 1941 at 1158). James, in fact, viewed the adoption of a comprehensive compensation plan for automobile accidents to be inevitable, a view of significant personal importance to his career. In a speech in 1939, just as the country was recovering from the Depression, James revealed,

> The feeling that automobile compensation would inevitably come in our generation so pervaded the rank and file of lawyers of my own city [New York] that it became a material factor in my decision to quit the active full-time practice of tort law.[4]

Of course, James' criticism of the fault system and his endorsement of a compensation plan were hardly novel. As earlier described, the 1932 Columbia Automobile Accident Report had documented the failure of the tort system to provide compensation to accident victims, especially the poor, and had recommended an insurance plan. James alluded to the committee's findings throughout his career and, at a later point, attempted to replicate the study (James & Law 1952). Many other scholars, of course, had included risk distribution as a relevant factor to be considered in accident cases (Y. Smith 1923 at 458–459; Feezer 1930; Gregory 1932). James, however, viewed risk distribution to be the only relevant factor, and the broader the distribution, the better. Thus James advocated a compensation system supported by general taxation rather than by specific levies on individual activities adjusted to the level of accidents they generate (James 1939, 1941). Although James often described his proposals in terms consistent with Bohlen's benefit theory or with the internalization theories of the time (James 1938), James believed that careful internalization of costs was of substantially less importance than broad risk distribution.

James' more specific ideas and something of his intellectual style were anticipated by William O. Douglas, who was perhaps a personal influence on James.

3 James 1941 at 1156. James hedged on this question in the Utah Speech (1939 at 210).

4 James 1939 at 210. Prior to entering teaching, James practiced as a personal injury defense lawyer for the New Haven Railroad.

In two brilliant articles published in 1929 (Douglas 1929a, 1929b), Douglas criticized Young B. Smith's "entrepreneur theory" of vicarious liability, which provided, simply, that entrepreneurs ought to pay all costs associated with their businesses because they can absorb the costs and pass them along to consumers in the prices of their products (Y. Smith 1923). According to Smith's theory, in the various contexts of vicarious liability—the negligence of a servant, an independent contractor, or one of a group of partners, for example—liability should be assigned according to indicia of entrepreneurial status: control over the productive activity, ownership of productive assets, investment at risk, and potential for profit. Smith had shown that common law rules of vicarious liability seemed to be sensitive to many of the concerns of entrepreneurial behavior, in particular to risk allocation, although he argued that the law could be made a great deal more coherent if the determinants of entrepreneurial status were more explicitly considered in defining legal rules (Y. Smith 1923).

Douglas argued that Smith's theory did not sufficiently focus on the risk-bearing capacity of the parties to the dispute (Douglas 1929a). Douglas claimed that risk-bearing capacity was the single most important consideration in these cases because it determined what the ultimate effect of a legal rule would be. Douglas criticized Smith's efforts carefully to attribute accident costs to one entrepreneurial activity or another by presenting a variety of examples in which differential defendant capacity to bear risks appeared to overwhelm differences in Smith's features of entrepreneurial status, such as control of the harm-causing activity. As an example, an independent contractor in control of operations may have only 100 customers over whom the burden could be spread, while the general contractor not in control of operations may have thousands of customers (Douglas 1929a at 595). Douglas argued that the complex rules and distinctions of vicarious liability law were incoherent in the modern world because they were introduced into the common law at a time when there were no standardized risk-shifting devices available in the marketplace (Douglas 1929a at 591). As a consequence, even those distinctions in the law that seemed related to appropriate risk allocation would probably disappear if more detailed social and economic studies of the parties' risk-bearing capacities, derived largely from nonlegal materials, were conducted (Douglas 1929a at 603).

Fleming James adopted the same scholarly approach, but added a persistence and a critical edge absent from Douglas' work. James immediately distinguished himself from other tort scholars of the time by the unrelenting character of his criticism of the fault system. The Columbia Automobile Accident Report had expressed some skepticism about how well the fault system achieved a compensation goal (Y. Smith 1932 at 797). James, in contrast, attacked every single feature of the fault system from his crystalline concern with assuring compensation to plaintiffs and distributing accident losses as broadly as possible.

An early article that seems to have propelled James into prominence demonstrates his style. In a 1941 *Harvard Law Review* piece, James criticized a proposal of the famous tort scholar Charles O. Gregory to allow contribution among joint tortfeasors.[5] Gregory endorsed contribution as a reform of the "evils of the rigid common-law system" of several liability. Gregory argued that imposing the damage burden on only one of a group of defendants was inconsistent with "any well-ordered and fair system of loss distribution."[6] Gregory's point, put simply, was that contribution was a superior rule because it spread losses to all defendants.

In a sharply worded criticism, James showed that Gregory had been insufficiently rigorous in his analysis of risk distribution.[7] According to James, contribution would impair rather than enhance risk distribution. Plaintiffs recovering judgments under joint and several liability routinely seek recovery first, and usually entirely, against that joint tortfeasor with the greatest assets or the most extensive operations. James saw this collection preference as serving an important social function because larger and richer defendants are in a better position to distribute losses broadly. In contrast, Gregory's contribution rule would apportion some of the damages to defendants less able to distribute risks and, in some cases, to judgment-proof defendants, preventing risk distribution altogether.[8]

Gregory attempted to mount a defense[9] but was obviously overwhelmed by James' attack. Gregory seems to have expected criticism of his contribution proposal from more traditional lawyers resistant to changing the ancient common-law prohibition on contribution and indifferent to the benefits of risk distribution. James, of course, was hostile to the common law and had strongly endorsed risk distribution. Gregory's position, thus, was savaged by one whom he had expected to be an ally. Gregory, like other tort scholars James influenced over his career, was forced to acknowledge lamely that James had simply thought through the problem more thoroughly and had accurately described the implications of Gregory's own approach:

> If Mr. James supported a program of socialization of loss through taxation or compulsory insurance, preferably administered by quasi-judicial commissions, I would be most sympathetic. This might mean complete abandonment of tort law as we have known it, which is not necessarily a condemnation.[10]

5 James 1941. James was responding to Gregory 1938. James had earlier criticized Gregory's book proposing contribution—see James 1936—and had also taken on Gregory in James 1939. Each of these articles was devoted to the contribution question.

6 Gregory 1938 at 373.

7 See generally James 1941.

8 James 1941 at 1165–1166. Also see James 1939 at 212. Note that James is presuming here a rigid form of comparative fault as opposed to strict contribution between tortfeasors.

9 Gregory 1941.

10 Gregory 1941 at 1171. Gregory, however, proceeds to criticize James for not specifically proposing a compensation system and for the implication of James' criticism that it is appropriate to take from the rich to subsidize the poor (*id.*).

James' advocacy of a compensation system alternative to tort law judgments became increasingly strident until 1950, when he announced support for absolute liability for accident losses.[11] There were few to concur with this extreme position, but the cumulative effect of James' work toward a growing consensus in the analysis of law on the importance of risk distribution ought not be underestimated.

James' scholarship after 1940 represents a calculated program aimed at achieving the complete overturn of the fault system and the substitution of a general accident compensation plan. There were two separate theaters of James' effort: first, he conducted a rule-by-rule assault on the fault system, indicating how the system's various features failed to distribute risks adequately while urging the extension of those features that increased the likelihood of recovery. Second, James systematically attempted to undermine the presuppositions of the fault system by demonstrating—largely with primitive empirical evidence—that the system had no deterrent effect on accident-causing behavior and that the accident rate was more likely to be reduced by the adoption of a compensation system. This was the beginning of economic analysis.

James' attack on those rules of the common law that reduced the likelihood of plaintiffs' recovery was relentless. He attacked the governmental and charitable immunities.[12] He proposed abolition of the defenses of assumption of risk,[13] contributory negligence,[14] and proximate cause.[15] He was critical of the last clear chance rule despite its role in defeating the contributory negligence defense, because it validated the mistaken belief that it was worth drawing fine distinctions between the fault of the parties.[16] James supported a comparative negligence rule, but unenthusiastically: as a doctrine transitional from the win-all, lose-all character of the fault system toward a more comprehensive system of social insurance.[17] James drew on substantial historical research in each of these articles, but the historical treatment was always the same. He showed how the fault-based focus of a rule was a feature of medieval times and that the modern direction of the law was toward liability without fault, with *Rylands v. Fletcher* and the workers' compensation plans as the most prominent models.[18] With these articles, James sought to devalue the common law of torts in favor of a functional approach.

11 James & Dickinson 1950.

12 James 1946.

13 James 1952.

14 James 1953.

15 James 1938.

16 *Id.*

17 *Id.* at 716.

18 For example, James 1938; James 1939 at 208–210; James 1946 at 366–370; James 1949. A large majority of James' articles include a litany of the wide range of areas in which non-fault liability is increasing; in these, James relies extensively and repeatedly on Nixon 1936 (Nixon wrote this paper when he was a third-year law student at Duke Law School).

As long as the fault system was retained, James endorsed the granting of more complete discretion over tort issues to juries, in contrast to the formulation of rigid legal rules or presumptions such as Holmes' "stop, look, listen" rule.[19] James preferred juries because he believed them to be more inclined to grant judgment to plaintiffs; rules and presumptions provided grounds for judicial dismissals of actions or directed verdicts against plaintiffs.[20] In yet another series of articles, James urged elevation of the role of the jury in accident cases on political grounds, because the views of jurors about compensation ought to be given more weight in a democracy than the views of judges, and because jurors were more sensitive to the determinants of the behavior of the average person.[21]

Each of James' criticisms of specific rules was accompanied by a discussion of psychological and physiological sources of accident-causing behavior, skeptical of the relevance of personal fault.[22] James devoted several additional articles, however, to more detailed and specific behavioral analyses. In a brilliant article published in 1950, James reviewed an extensive industrial psychology literature that appeared to prove that the very large majority of accidents were caused by accident-prone persons.[23] One study of industrial accidents estimated that 10 percent of the work force was involved in 75 percent of workplace accidents;[24] another claimed that 4 percent of drivers was involved in one-third of all auto accidents.[25] James prominently cited the conclusion of one of these studies (in this and in many succeeding articles): "Recent medical research has shown that 'accident proneness' may be an innate characteristic of some individuals and a personal phenomenon independent of any question of responsibility, conscious action or blameworthiness."[26]

James believed it important to his program to address carefully the relative deterrent effects of fault and compensation systems, an economic point. In a 1948 article he claimed that the most important determinants of accident avoidance were the fear of personal injury to the actor himself and the tremendous incidental costs of an accident in terms of the disruption of the victim's life that were neither compensated by the fault system nor by any proposed

19 In a case involving an accident at a railway crossing, Holmes had ruled that the driver of a car had an obligation to "stop, look and listen" before crossing the tracks. *Baltimore & Ohio R.R. Co.*
20 James 1938 at 717.
21 For example, 1949, 1950.
22 1938 at 709–714, 1939 at 210, 1941 at 1157–1159, 1948; James & Dickinson 1950.
23 1950.
24 *Id.* at 770 (Bristol study).
25 *Id.* at 769–770 (Blain study).
26 James & Dickinson 1950 at 775 (citing Bristol). James felt a great deal of uneasiness about introducing this form of evidence because of its benefit to defendants invoking a contributory negligence defense. James argued in James & Dickinson 1950 that defendants ought not be allowed to introduce evidence of this nature as a matter of law. He proposed that, if the fault system were to be retained, the defendant's negligence should be judged on an objective standard set according to the reasonableness of the average defendant, while the plaintiff's contributory negligence should be judged according to a subjective standard personal to the plaintiff itself (*id.* at 784–787).

insurance system.[27] James cited an estimate that these incidental costs were four times the magnitude of the direct compensable costs of personal injury; again, a sign of economic thinking.[28]

James attempted to prove that the best methods to prevent accidents were safety programs[29] coupled with therapeutic care or more selective job placement for the accident-prone.[30] James believed that such programs were more likely to be initiated if large enterprises were made responsible for all accident losses.[31]

> Since the large business or governmental unit is in a far better position to reduce accidents than is the isolated individual, and since absolute liability puts added pressure to reduce accidents on the large unit, it follows that absolute liability will be a greater spur to safety than a system of less strict liability.[32]

James claimed that, after workers' compensation systems had been adopted, insurance companies along with employers instituted safety-awareness programs.[33] In James' view, these programs were responsible for the decline in the rate of industrial accidents after World War II in contrast to the absence of change in the rate of automobile accidents over the same period, an explicitly economic conclusion.[34]

Finally, James (following Douglas) argued that, although the rules of the fault system appeared relatively constant, they were being quietly rendered obsolete by the institution of insurance. The practical effects of common-law rules differed according to the insurance coverage of the parties to accidents and according to the distinctions enforced by insurance carriers in the policies they offer.[35] "[T]he practices of the carriers have become just as much rules of law as the pronouncements of the courts interpreting traditional doctrines."[36] James believed that the fault system of tort law had become epiphenomenal to the accident problem. Yet the spread of private market insurance, while growing, remained incomplete. Many victims of accidents, particularly the poor, were themselves uninsured or were injured by uninsured tortfeasors.[37] The system should be repudiated explicitly and immediately.

27 James 1948.
28 *Id.* at 558 (citing *Bests' Insurance Rev.*).
29 *Id.* at 559–563.
30 James & Dickinson 1950 at 776–777.
31 James 1948 at 550–51; James & Dickinson 1950, at 779–780.
32 1950 at 780.
33 James 1948 at 559–561.
34 *Id.* at 561–562. Also see James & Thornton 1950 at 441.
35 *Id.*
36 *Id.* at 431.
37 James 1948 at 564, 568.

Although James' scholarship is noteworthy for its sheer analytic power, almost all of his articles incorporate extensive reference to empirical studies, several conducted by James himself.[38] James apparently believed that it was crucial to his program to demonstrate that his proposals for society-wide risk distribution were supported by facts. The data source that defined the issues for the entire generation of scholarship was the 1932 Columbia Auto Compensation Report documenting the large proportion of victims, most commonly the poor, who received no compensation whatsoever for their accident losses, whether from tortfeasors or first-party insurance.[39] James made constant reference to the report's findings throughout his writings. In his criticism of Gregory's proposal to allow contribution among joint tortfeasors, James conducted a different empirical study of his own. He collected a sample of cases from jurisdictions allowing contribution and wrote to the attorneys involved to discover what the compensation record had been. Consistent with his theory, he found that the contribution rule "tends to favor the large and wealthy at the expense of the relatively poor and weak," and thus was ineffective as a technique of risk distribution.[40]

In another article, James presented extensive evidence of the sources of accidents,[41] as well as of ultimate accident rates in various contexts, with and without private insurance, before and after the adoption of compensation systems.[42] In 1952, James duplicated the Columbia auto accident study with data drawn from New Haven examining how the problem of undercompensation had changed in the succeeding thirty years.[43] He found only modest improvement. The most important discovery of the Columbia study had been the low percentage of victims able to obtain adequate recovery from uninsured drivers. In 1932, only 15 percent obtained adequate recovery; James found that in 1952, twenty years later, only 22 percent obtained adequate recovery.[44] James also found no significant difference between the two periods in the likelihood of suffering injury from an uninsured driver.[45] These findings again confirmed to James the need for either compulsory private insurance or a general compensation plan.

James, as I have mentioned, was the dominant tort scholar of the period. No other scholar compares to James in the range of tort problems addressed, with the possible exception of Prosser in the largely derivative first edition of his

38 The exceptions are those written for his treatise with Fowler Harper, which make only incidental reference to empirical studies.

39 Committee 1932.

40 James 1941 at 1165.

41 James & Dickinson 1950.

42 *Id.*; James 1948; James & Thornton 1950.

43 James & Law 1952.

44 *Id.* at 75.

45 *Id.* at 74.

hornbook.[46] Throughout the period, many of James' criticisms of the fault system had substantial scholarly support.[47] For example, virtually every commentator recommended the adoption of comparative negligence in place of the absolute bar of contributory negligence.[48]

James' principal influence, however, was the increasing acceptance in legal scholarship of the relevance of risk distribution to the accident problem, the result of his unceasing advocacy. In the early years, aside from James, risk distribution was only occasionally discussed;[49] a significant group of authors ignored the issue,[50] and some—Paul Leidy is an example—believed risk distribution to be alien to common-law values.[51] As the years progressed, however, risk distribution advanced to become a central consideration in the large majority of articles,[52] most citing various parts of the James corpus. It was now the exceptional article that ignored risk distribution,[53] and even those few scholars, like Prosser, who regarded risk distribution as of secondary importance felt obliged to discuss the subject at length.[54] This represents the growing triumph of the functional approach to law.

None of James' contemporaries, however, ever fully accepted James' single focus on risk distribution. From my readings, most scholars were convinced by James' strong (although to my mind controversial) argument that the societal gains from risk distribution outweigh any specific deterrent effect of damage judgments. And there were certainly no refutations of the centrality of risk distribution considerations, nor—except for Leidy—were there even suggestions that the principle must be limited in some way. Yet one can sense in the literature some unstated reluctance to wholesale commitment to risk distribution as an objective. Throughout the mid-1940s, James' approach to tort problems remained radical, at the very least on the fringe of theory.

I believe that the reluctance to accept risk distribution as the only consideration of relevance in accident cases stemmed from the continuing influence of the economic internalization concept. The principle of cost internalization was central to the mainstream analysis of the accident problem during the entire period of James' work.[55] I am certain that James perceived that the careful internalization of costs to activities that give rise to them can often conflict with distributing risks most broadly, in particular where neither of the parties to the

46 Prosser 1941.

47 Nixon 1936; Cooley 1941; Gregory 1941; Morris 1952.

48 MacIntyre 1940; Cooley 1941; Gregory 1941; Prosser 1948.

49 Feezer 1930; 1931; Cooley 1941; Gregory 1941.

50 See, for example, MacIntyre 1940; Eldredge 1941.

51 Leidy 1940.

52 Commission 1943, at 413; Friedmann 1949; Morris 1952; Green 1953.

53 See McNiece & Thornton 1949.

54 See Prosser 1943; Prosser's aversion to risk distribution is elaborated in White 1980.

55 Thayer 1916; Green 1928; Feezer 1930, 1931; Gregory 1932; Smith 1932; Bohlen 1937; Sabel 1938; Prosser 1943; Morris 1952.

dispute is an insurer or a large enterprise. Throughout his career, as a result, James minimized the importance of strict internalization in favor of general social insurance. But few followed this direction of James. Perhaps tort scholars were convinced by the (pre-Coasian) economic theory of externalities; perhaps by some lingering sense of the justness of attributing costs to specific activities (a point that Posner, *infra* Chapter 7, will exploit and redefine). Throughout the entire period, however, no single scholar, not even James, convincingly criticized the notion of internalization.

The continuing success of the internalization idea also may have accounted for the reluctance of the profession to abandon the fault system, despite James' multiple and eventually uncontested criticisms of it. Over the entire period, I have found no defense of the fault system on grounds other than maintaining stability in the law.[56] Yet the common-law system of damages does serve to internalize costs to specific activities. Perhaps it was the internalization principle that kept the legal community from joining James' total repudiation.

James' advocacy of increasingly strict and finally absolute liability seems closely related to our modern law of products liability. In fact, James was uninterested in the subject of liability for defective products until very late in his career. Indeed, the subject of manufacturer or retailer liability for defective products was of minor scholarly significance during the 1930s and 1940s. The first rank of torts and contracts scholars only touched on the subject in their efforts to be encyclopedic;[57] the major figures of the "field" were Lester Feezer, A.J. Russell, and Lindsey Jeanblanc, whose efforts today are hardly known.[58] During the period, virtually all discussions—building on Cardozo's opinion in *MacPherson* 1916—recommended the extension of negligence liability to all products causing personal injury,[59] although there were small debates over manufacturer versus retailer liability.[60] There was consistent criticism of the doctrine of privity of contract.[61] Indeed, I have discovered only one commentator during the period Leidy—who defended privity of contract, but even he proceeded also to support the extension of negligence liability in defective product cases.[62]

The problem of central importance to James and to the major tort scholars of his generation was the consequences of automobile accidents, largely because of the empirical magnitude of the losses.[63] James, of course, wanted to extend the absolute liability solution of workers' compensation to auto accidents. But it is obvious that the extension is highly problematic. It is difficult to see how the

56 Lilly 1932.
57 See Goodhart 1935.
58 Russell 1933; Feezer & Campbell 1935; Jeanblanc 1937.
59 Feezer 1931; Russell 1933; Feezer 1938; Eldredge 1943 at 390.
60 See Russell 1933; Feezer 1938.
61 Bohlen 1905a, 1905b; Feezer 1931; Winfield 1934; Seavey 1939.
62 Leidy 1942. But see Bohlen's defense of *Winterbottom v. Wright* in Bohlen 1905a at 281–283.
63 For the magnitude of automobile accident losses, see James & Law 1952.

relationship of colliding drivers resembles the workplace relationship of employers and employees. Perhaps where a driver has struck a pedestrian the analogy is closer.[64] But which of the parties to a two-car collision is to be made absolutely liable? This conundrum explains why James pressed so vigorously for a general compensation system supported by taxation disregarding the careful internalization of costs to specific activities.

James' sustained advocacy of risk distribution as opposed to the age-old principles of the common law accelerated the shift after the Depression to the acceptance of the functional approach to law. Though James was at the forefront, many other scholars began debating how, if the common law was to be replaced, it should be done.

Because the largest volume of accidental losses in the society at the time was traffic accidents, most of these proposals dealt with auto accident compensation plans. A plethora of studies and plans were proposed, all rejecting the common law of torts and accepting the functional approach.

Perhaps the most prominent study—sealing the functional approach to law—was by (my dear late teachers) Walter J. Blum and Harry Kalven, Jr.: *Public Law Perspectives on a Private Law Problem* (1964). Their title demonstrates the new approach, shifting from the principles of the common law to public law analysis.

> Torts has been regarded as a private law topic concerned with resolving the disputes between particular individuals. But when the one turns to insurance funds and compensation plans, the matter becomes alchemized into large public law dealing with large groups in the society.[65]

Blum and Kalven defined the purpose of automobile compensation plans in strictly functional terms: The

> two main targets [of compensation plans are] the elimination of … the gap in common law coverage [the gap was injuries from single car accidents victims themselves and the negligent who had to bear their own losses] and a dramatic improvement of the timing of payments to victims.[66]

They adopted "the idea of treating the tort system as performing [a] social welfare purpose."[67]

This was still not the arrival of law and economics. Blum and Kalven conceded economic approaches to the problem,[68] but analyzed them as limited:

64 James frequently used auto-pedestrian collisions as examples for his points, as did his protégé Calabresi, discussed *infra*, Chapter 6.

65 Blum & Kalven 1964 at 646.

66 *Id.* at 669.

67 *Id.* at 675.

68 *Id.* at 696.

> the idiom of economic analysis has been widely imported into legal literature in what now strikes us as being an incomplete and confusing way. … [Lawyers] hear the economist talking about proper and improper allocation of costs and understand him as saying that an improper allocation of costs leads to an uneconomic and impolitic result. The lawyer's expectation is that by translating the liability issue into a question of costs, he can draw on the expertise of the economist to reach a proper allocation of those costs.
>
> But if the economist is patient and candid, the lawyer will find his great expectations shaken. The economist will point out that the allocation of costs is not a matter of giving a description of the facts of the economic order, as the lawman seems to have thought. Rather the allocation of costs is always avowedly instrumental.[69]

The functional approach to law was taking hold.

69 By which I believe they meant designed to achieve some instrumental end (*id.* at 696, 695). As we shall see in Chapter 6, Calabresi takes this point much further.

4

THE BIRTH OF MODERN LAW AND ECONOMICS AS A DISCIPLINE

James's work contained some economic insights. Other work in the era showed some appreciation of economic ideas, in particular the internalization of costs idea to appropriately set the marginal costs of an activity. But these were simple economic ideas.

The more serious study of law and economics began at Chicago. To my knowledge, the University of Chicago Law School was the first to grant tenure to an economist: to Henry Simons in 1939; next to Aaron Director (Figure 4.1) in 1949.[1] One might think that the appointments of Simons and Director represented a prescient appreciation of the gains from integrating the two disciplines or, at the least, an important interdisciplinary experiment. There is some truth to this point. The immediate motivation for Simons' appointment, however, was different. The University of Chicago Law School initiated a four-year law curriculum in the 1930s in which students without a BA could accelerate their studies leading to a law degree in four years (Kitch 1983 at 166). It was evident to the planners of the program that law students without a BA would need to have complementary courses to build their education along with formal law courses. The social sciences, including economics, accounting, sociology, and criminology, were practical examples. This apparently led to the appointment of Henry Simons to the Law School in 1939 (Kitch 1983 at 167, 168, 189).

There was another aspect to Simons' appointment to the Law School. He was regarded as a fertile mind but had written very little: at the time of his Law School appointment, two book reviews. He probably would have been denied

1 Kitch 1983. The Law School had a long interest in social sciences: It had appointed the political scientist Ernst Freund to the faculty in 1892.

tenure in the economics department.[2] Thus, his appointment preserved the publication standard of the Chicago Economics Department.[3]

The appointment of Director to the Law School, some years later, was different. Director had been brought to Chicago in 1947 after the University had accepted funds from an organization called the Volker Fund[4] for the study of capitalism and private enterprise.[5] Director later continued as the central figure in the Law School's Antitrust Project, also principally supported by outside funds.

FIGURE 4.1 Aaron Director
Photo courtesy of the University of Chicago Law School

2 *Id.* at 174. See also Coase 1993a at 243.

3 Curiously, other members of the economics department, including some usually regarded as opponents of today's Chicago School approach, seem to have participated more in the life of the law school in the early years. Paul Douglas published an article in the *University of Chicago Law Review* in 1946; Hayek and Knight published in 1948 and 1949; Douglas published yet a further article in 1951. For a description of the conflicting approaches of Chicago economists, see Reder 1982.

4 *See* Kitch 1983 at 180. The Volker Fund was also instrumental in supporting the Mont Pelerin Society (Hartwell 1995 at 104, 45–46).

5 Apparently other universities had refused to accept this money (Kitch 1983 at 181, 187). Hayek also came to Chicago as a result of the Volker Fund money (*id.* at 187). Aaron Director was instrumental in convincing the University of Chicago Press to publish Hayek's *Road to Serfdom* (Coase 1993a at 244–247).

The University of Chicago Law School in this period, and in the period shortly after, was highly entrepreneurial. The Antitrust Project was one of three major research efforts and, of the three, the least auspicious. More prominent and more prominently funded were Harry Kalven's Jury Project[6] and Soia Mentschikoff's Arbitration Project.

In retrospect, the Antitrust Project has had the greatest intellectual influence by far. The single enduring product of the Jury Project is Kalven and Zeisel's *The American Jury*, which, though it still provides the best information available about the substance of jury decisions, shows only that we are unable to distinguish trial by jury very clearly from trial by judge in terms of plaintiff/defendant success rates, both around 50 percent, which Kalven and Zeisel viewed as justifying the jury system.[7] The Arbitration Project produced, to my knowledge, nothing.[8] The intellectual output of Director's Antitrust Project, on the other hand, continues to account for our leading theories of industrial behavior. I can think of only one area of antitrust analysis—information exchanges—in which the dominant theories today do not derive from Director or Director's Project.[9]

Director's Project was largely, though not entirely, centered on papers published in the *Journal of Law & Economics*, which began publication in 1958. Looking back on those efforts, law and economics, as developed by Director and his successor as Editor Ronald Coase, was not exactly ideological, but derived from what might be called a deeply-held belief system that political interference in market activities interfered with freedom and reduced societal welfare. The phrase "reduced societal welfare" is a modern, technocratic concept. The opposition of Director and Coase to governmental interference in market activities was much deeper. Director was one of the founding members (along with Milton Friedman, Frank Knight, von Mises, and George Stigler, among others) of the Mont Pelerin Society, organized by Friedrich Hayek in 1946. Hayek had published *The Road to Serfdom* in 1944. Following themes of *The Road to Serfdom*, the Mont Pelerin Society was, and to some extent still is, dedicated to the proposition that political interference with market activities is harmful to freedom (though the Society avoided a purely libertarian approach) and to broader individual and societal goals. Coase was not present at the first

6 The Jury Project brought the sociologist Hans Zeisel to the Law School Like Director, Zeisel was later elevated to a tenured position.

7 Priest and Klein, both at one-time Fellows in the successor Antitrust Project directed by Coase, later established a theoretical basis for why this might be true, based on the behavior of litigants selecting when to settle cases (Priest & Klein 1984).

8 I believe that Mentschikoff's famous arbitration paper preceded the grant (Soia Mentschikoff 1952). Perhaps it formed the basis for the application. At a later point, Soia Mentschikoff offered me the data compiled by the Arbitration Project, and asked me to analyze it and write up the findings of the surveys of arbitration practices that she and her associates had compiled years earlier. She sent me the boxes of data. I looked at them and found them entirely unintelligible.

9 Director's ideas about vertical integration remain dominant, though complemented by the recent work of Williamson, Klein, and Alchian on opportunism and the theory of the firm.

meeting of the Society but became a member two years later, in 1948, at the behest of Hayek (Priest 2014a) and, at some later point, a Life Member. Besides indirect influence on Director and, perhaps, others, Hayek's important work has had little influence on modern law and economics.

The early volumes of the *Journal of Law & Economics* illustrate the commitment of the editors to the belief in the superiority of the market to political allocation of resources. The first issues contain some articles that might be regarded as economic science, but contain numerous articles that are essentially essays in political economy—market-oriented political economy: in Volume 2 of the *Journal*, Hirschleifer's articles "Capitalist Ethics—Tough or Soft"[10] and "The Sumptuary Manifesto,"[11] and Buchanan's "Positive Economics, Welfare Economics, and Political Economy;"[12] in Volume 3, Jacob Viner's "The Intellectual History of Laissez Faire;"[13] in Volume 4, Stigler's "Private Vice and Public Virtue."[14] Though these early volumes of the *Journal* do not ignore the scientific application of economic analysis, they resemble more closely a high-level journal of pro-market political philosophy than a journal of economic science.

The political philosophy, however, would not entirely generate the law and economics movement; the philosophy combined with empirical work would. From the earliest issues, the editors—Director and Coase—encouraged articles critical of specific governmental interventions in the market, first to complement, later to completely supplant, the essays on political economy.

Antitrust law and economic regulation were particular subjects of criticism, though articles in the *Journal* also addressed the effects, economic and otherwise, of the minimum wage,[15] unionization,[16] licensing,[17] and even the British National Health Service,[18] among others.

In the first issue of the *Journal*, Director published John McGee's reanalysis of the *Standard Oil* case, showing that the basic theory of predatory pricing as one of the elements of the Supreme Court's opinion finding Standard Oil guilty of violating the Sherman Act had misunderstood the economic practices at issue entirely.[19] According to Director's view, Rockefeller and associates had created the Standard Oil monopoly not by predatory practices such as undercutting

10 Hirshleifer 1959.

11 Hirshleifer 1959.

12 Buchanan 1959. Buchanan became a member of Mont Pelerin somewhat later, in 1957; subsequently, a Life Member.

13 Viner 1960.

14 Stigler 1961.

15 Colberg 1960; Brozen 1962.

16 Many articles in the early volumes addressed the effects of unions; e.g., Rees 1959; Lurie 1960. The entirety of Volume 6 was devoted to studies of unionization.

17 Moore 1961.

18 Lees 1962 ("the N.H.S. [is] incompatible in important ways, … with the basic assumptions of a free society").

19 McGee 1958.

prices, but by buying out rivals, giving them a share of potential monopoly profits.[20] Note that the point of McGee's argument is not that the Standard Oil monopoly was not a monopoly and, perhaps, ripe for dissolution (McGee expressly put aside that question), but rather that the economic analysis of predatory pricing adopted by the Supreme Court and in popular understanding was naïve, if not idiotic. McGee's point, surely encouraged by Director,[21] was to demonstrate that the justification given by the Court and accepted in popular opinion for governmental interference in this famous case was essentially nonsense.

Most of the other articles criticizing antitrust law solicited or encouraged by Director and Coase were of this nature: Telser's study of resale price maintenance, criticizing the Supreme Court's *General Electric* opinion;[22] Ward Bowman's[23] and later Ken Dam's[24] work on tying arrangements; Stigler's article on the *U.S. Steel* case;[25] John Peterman's studies of *Brown Shoe* and, later, *International Salt*;[26] Bowman's later study of predatory pricing.[27] Although these articles generated substantial new learning concerning industrial practices, the underlying aim of the antitrust program was only partially scientific advance; more centrally, to ridicule the grounds upon which courts interfered with the marketplace. Because this new economic approach departed so greatly from then-current Supreme Court opinions, the tone of the work was often extreme, in many cases sarcastic, rather than an effort to sensitively educate the Court or to recommend marginal changes to Supreme Court positions.[28]

The Antitrust Project was, perhaps, the most successful research program in the history of legal scholarship. Director was able to bring to the program a highly able set of researchers including John Jewkes, William Letwin, McGee, Robert Bork, Paul MacAvoy, and Ward Bowman.[29] But more remarkable was the coherence of the Project as an intellectual effort. The Antitrust Project supported or inspired:

20 My later study of Standard Oil found that Standard Oil was able to buy out rivals because of the rebates it could obtain from railroads by increasing the capacity of the freight loads Standard Oil could promise (Priest 2012).

21 McGee credits Director for the basic analysis of the economic superiority of acquisition to predatory price cutting as a means of creating a monopoly (McGee 1958).

22 Telser 1960.

23 Bowman 1957.

24 Dam 1969.

25 Stigler 1965, also influenced by Director; see Kitch 1983 at 207.

26 Peterman 1975a, 1975b; 1979.

27 Bowman 1967.

28 Ronald Coase explained that his recollection of the antitrust course "was what I would call 'hearty laughter.' We'd read what these people were saying, and we couldn't make any sense of it at all. It was just absurd what was going on" (Kitch 1983).

29 Coase 1988 at 247.

1. Letwin's (1965) book on the common law of restraint of trade and the history of the Sherman Act, still the best available source;
2. the work of MacAvoy (1965) and McGee (1960) on cartel behavior—MacAvoy's book remains a classic;
3. Director and Levi's (1956) seminal article on exclusionary practices;
4. McGee (1958) on predatory pricing;
5. Bowman (1955) and Telser (1960) on resale price maintenance, and Stone (1963) on other distributional restraints;
6. McGee (1960) on monopolization;
7. Bowman's (1957) famous article on tying arrangements;
8. McGee (1966) and Bowman (1973) on patent license arrangements;
9. Jewkes et al. (1958) on the sources of innovation;
10. Bork (1954) and Bowman (1955, 1957) on vertical integration, with the related work of the Hales (Hale & Hale 1958, 1962; Hale 1967), fellow travelers;
11. McGee (1956) and Dam (1963) on price discrimination;
12. the work of Jewkes (1953, 1958) and McGee (1964) on government regulation of business.[30]

Finally, the members of the Project were sufficiently conscious of the importance of their efforts to generate their own propaganda. Robert Bork (1968) in a reanalysis of the legislative history of the Sherman Act argued powerfully (ignoring Letwin) that Congress in 1890 possessed a view about restraint of trade identical to that that the Chicago School was to develop in the 1960s. It is an unstated implication of this clever and influential paper that to understand the original intent of Senator Sherman and the 51st Congress, one should study the work of the Chicago Antitrust Project.

Of course, I have enumerated only the research of members directly supported by the Antitrust Project. The influence of Director (Figure 4.2) and of the community surrounding him on the industrial organization research of members of Chicago's Economics Department and Business School (such as Stigler and Telser) and on students (such as Dam, Peltzman, and Liebeler) is more difficult to document, but undoubtedly substantial. Director's most important intellectual contribution addressed the evaluation of vertical practices by firms. Quite in contrast to antitrust doctrine at the time, Director saw that it was impossible for a single firm to increase its market power unilaterally because it faced competition from other firms. Director, who himself wrote almost nothing, did not seem concerned about the prohibition of horizontal agreements

30 Director was responsible for other ideas that remain prominent. Most important is the identification of characteristics of industries that predispose toward collusion (see McGee 1960). This approach has been central to the antitrust work of Richard Posner as well as to the subsequent Areeda and Turner antitrust treatise.

FIGURE 4.2 Aaron Director and his group. Director (center); to the right, Robert Bork. Third from left, Ward Bowman. Next left, Henry Manne

Photo courtesy of the University of Chicago Law School

among competitors—such as price fixing. The articles that he encouraged dealt with vertical practices alleged to be anticompetitive, such as predatory pricing (McGee and Bowman); resale price maintenance (Telser and Bowman); tying arrangements (Bowman, Dam, and Peterman); alleged monopolization (McGee); vertical integration (Bork, Bowman, and the Hales); and price discrimination (McGee).

Director's ideas on these subjects had great influence. As shall be explained in Chapter 9, Bork's famous and influential book *The Antitrust Paradox* derives from Director's analysis of vertical versus horizontal practices (that then-current antitrust law treated these practices similarly constitutes the paradox). As shall also be explained, Director had broader intellectual influence. Prior to his appointment to the Supreme Court, John Paul Stevens taught with Director at the University of Chicago Law School, later describing their co-teaching as the most important intellectual experience of his life.

Director's work, as I have mentioned, has had a continuing influence on the analysis of industrial behavior. It is the most successful application of economics to problems raised by law in history. But the work of the Antitrust Project had little influence on the rise of law and economics in the 1960s and 1970s. In those years, economics would be put forth to explain the law more generally.

Director, in contrast, had no interest in the law or, for that matter, in legal problems. Director looked to antitrust cases as sources of evidence of industrial behavior. The records of these cases provided the raw data to be analyzed by the Project's members. The Justice Department and defense lawyers who had struggled to collect the data for trial and to compile them in usable form were unpaid research assistants. Often they had failed to collect the best data and, almost always, had failed to ask the right questions about the data. But the data were there. The role of the court's opinion at best was to provide a naïve theory to be disproved. The legal system was an additional example of a misguided public institution interfering with the market and private ordering. A few of the Project's essays were written with an eye toward law reform; Bork's contributions are the principal examples. But there is no evidence in the work of the Project of Director's interest in the law or in purely legal problems.

5

THE REVOLUTIONARY EXPANSION OF LAW AND ECONOMICS

Ronald H. Coase

The principal focus of law and economics at Chicago under Aaron Director on antitrust and government regulation would change and expand into a dominant analytical approach to all of law. This expansion developed in a very peculiar way: with Director's commissioning of an article on the regulation of broadcasting by the British economist Ronald H. Coase (Figure 5.1). Coase was a British scholar, though never affiliated with the major British universities. He was recruited to America first by the University of Buffalo in 1951, next by the University of Virginia Economics Department in 1958, and subsequently by Director to the University of Chicago Law School in 1964.

Coase was awarded the Nobel Prize in Economics in 1991, but he was not a trained economist: his undergraduate studies were in law and commerce.[1] He had no economics Ph.D. As a student, he became increasingly interested in industrial issues, and in 1931 was awarded a traveling scholarship to the United States which he spent visiting many industrial establishments to study, in his words, "lateral and vertical integration."[2] In 1937, at the age of 27, he published his earliest important paper, "The Nature of the Firm,"[3] based on his analysis of American industrial organization. The paper remains highly original and revealing of Coase's interest in and willingness to address fundamental questions at an early age. It discussed why firms are organized and how firm behavior relates to other market behavior. Since individual transactions in the market serve to

1 Most of Coase's illustrations of externality problems in "The Federal Communications Commission" and "The Problem of Social Cost" are drawn from English common-law cases. He has recounted that he was very interested in law and economics from courses taught at the London School of Economics by distinguished practicing attorneys (Kitch 1983 at 211–212).

2 Coase 2000.

3 Coase 1937.

FIGURE 5.1 Ronald Coase. To the left is Harold Demsetz
Photo courtesy of the University of Chicago Law School

allocate resources through their responses to price signals, why do firms exist that substitute administrative control for those market transactions? Why is there integration in a firm at all, rather than complete reliance on market transactions through the price system?

Coase's answer is that the existence of firms must demonstrate that there are costs of entering into market transactions, costs that can be reduced by administrative allocative decisions within firms. Coase gives an example of these cost savings (this is a paraphrase): through the market, a worker moves from job X to job Y as a result of being drawn by a wage (price) differential as between X and Y. In contrast, in a firm, a worker moves from Division X to Division Y, not as a result of a price differential as between X and Y, "but because he is ordered to do so."[4]

In this example, the worker's manager supersedes the price mechanism by making an allocative decision, presumably (implied by Coase) authorized to do so because of the price savings of an administrative decision over the costs of using relative market pricing to influence the decision of the worker to move from X to Y.

4 Coase 1937 at 35.

Coase defines that the principal function of the manager is to discover what relative prices would be and possesses a comparative advantage (these are my terms) because he or she can do so at a lower cost than can individuals in the market. Thus, the manager knows or believes that the value of the worker at Division Y is greater than the value at Division X, and reallocates the worker's efforts appropriately. Coase provides no analysis as to how this is done; the relatively cheaper cost of administrative control is presumed from the existence of the firm.

Coase does not emphasize the point, but his argument can be put in terms of information. In Coase's example about the operation of the firm, the manager has differentially superior information about the relative productivity of inputs to production to outweigh the costs of using price information developed through a market process to determine allocation.

This point is related to other analyses of the importance of information to explaining the function of the market, in particular the analyses of the Austrian school, led by Hayek and von Mises. Coase, in writing "The Nature of the Firm," was not an Austrian. In the paper (again, published when he was 27), in the manner of an excellent student, he thoroughly discusses the literature relevant to the issue, ranging broadly from discussions of the nature of economic science to the economic assumptions underlying the understanding of the market. Coase does not rely on the Austrians. Coase cites Hayek once, but criticizes Hayek's emphasis on the centrality of the price system for generating information, which might be expected since Coase focuses on the role of the manager of the firm in supplanting the price system. Coase recounts that, as a student, he attended lectures of Hayek and that Hayek was instrumental in firming up the theoretical analysis of the field.[5] Nevertheless, as a former student of Coase, I do not remember him ever referring to Hayek, von Mises, or other Austrians; certainly not emphasizing their work or showing conceptual similarities.[6]

Although later recognized as highly innovative, "The Nature of the Firm" seems to have had little impact at the time. It appears not to have influenced the industrial organization literature until discovered by the Chicago School in the late-1950s. Again, it seems not to have been recognized by the Austrians. Admittedly, it was written by a 27-year-old, with no prominent academic position. And Coase appears not to have followed up on the idea. To my knowledge, Coase published no further general articles on firm organization or behavior within a firm.[7]

5 Kitch 1983 at 217.

6 For a discussion of the relation between British economists and the work of the Austrians, see Tribe 2009 at 68 (arguing that British economists did not subscribe to the anti-statist views of the Austrians because they wanted to remain relevant to policy discussions in Britain's post-war planned economy).

7 Coase, for some period, published a column in an accounting journal which obliquely addressed issues of firm organization from a tax standpoint.

In subsequent years, Coase continued to work on industrial organization issues. In 1946, roughly a decade after "The Nature of the Firm," Coase published an article, "The Marginal Cost Controversy."[8] Coase addresses the argument, current then among prominent economists as he describes it, that prices for all services and commodities should be equal to marginal costs. This proposition of course was fully accepted by Coase with respect to increasing cost industries, and is the basis for the demonstration in economic theory of a maximum welfare equilibrium through unfettered market transactions. The more difficult question, addressed by Coase in this article, is how to deal with pricing in decreasing cost industries, such as public utilities: industries in which, at the current level of demand, the marginal costs of production are lower than average costs. This was a well-known problem in economic analysis, described in the nineteenth century as the "Railroad Problem." If, at the level of demand, the marginal cost per unit of output is lower than the average cost, the social welfare equilibrium where price equals marginal cost cannot sustain the enterprise. Though initially identified in the nineteenth century with respect to railroads, and thought then to extend more broadly to most manufacturing industries, in 1946 it was chiefly of interest with respect to public utilities.

Coase describes comprehensively that the prevailing approach among economists at the time was to conclude that, for industries of this nature, the government should make up the shortfall between prices set at marginal cost and necessary total revenue where prices would have to equal average cost to sustain the enterprise. According to this seeming economic consensus, the government should achieve this end through subsidies to decreasing cost industries paid for through general taxation.

Coase challenged this view. Coase argued, first, that consumers using a product or service, decreasing cost or otherwise, ought to be required to pay the full costs of its production. Coase was making an economic point: if consumers pay less than full costs, there will be overconsumption from a societal point of view of the product or service, though there seems to also have been a moral dimension to his emphasis.[9] He also pointed out that to support these subsidies required taxation of other societal activities that would lead to underconsumption, from a social welfare perspective, of the products, services, or activities taxed.[10] Second, Coase argued (and this was the heart of the paper) that there were other pricing mechanisms that could achieve, somewhat roughly, the marginal cost principle, but still return full revenues to the producer: multipart pricing most prominently.

8 Coase 1946.
9 See Coase 1988.
10 Note the similarity in this criticism to Coase's later criticism in "The Problem of Social Cost" of Pigou's proposals to impose taxes on activities generating externalities.

Coase, presumably encouraged by his mentor Arnold Plant,[11] next studied the monopoly of the British Broadcasting Corporation (BBC) over British telecommunications, later published as a book, *British Broadcasting: A Study in Monopoly* (Coase 1950).[12] In this work, Coase criticized the BBC's monopoly, asking why should a governmental agency possess a monopoly of broadcasting to the exclusion of other available private sources. Coase's criticism (which is muted in the book; it is centrally a detailed history of the establishment of the BBC monopoly) chiefly derives from freedom of speech and diversity of speech grounds: that the BBC, like all monopolies, reduces output and, in particular, does not cater to the interests of all citizens, favoring elite interests which an open market would not, and has actively suppressed speech where critical of government positions—as a prominent example, prior to World War II, refusing to broadcast Churchill's criticisms of the Munich Accords (Coase 1950 at 166, 189). Coase later did work in 1958 at the Center for Advanced Study at Stanford on U.S. Federal Communications Commission (FCC) regulation.[13]

Aaron Director, as Editor of the *Journal of Law & Economics*, was surely aware of Coase's initial work on British broadcasting and of his work at Stanford.[14] An idea at the time had been promoted among Chicago economists—I do not know its precise origin; it was principally promoted by Director (though it sounds like an idea of Director's brother-in-law, Milton Friedman)—that the hostility in the United States among political liberals to government regulation of broadcasting on free speech grounds could be exploited to convert these liberals to join the free-market, anti-governmental movement that Director was leading. Less concerned about monopoly (the United States had competing telecommunications networks), Director argued that, if liberals believed that government regulation of telecommunications is harmful, why should they not believe that governmental regulation of other industries in the society is harmful as well.[15] Thus, Director attempted to transform the opponents of government interference with free speech into allies against government interference in the economy more generally.

Coase was an implement to this strategy. Director encouraged Coase to write about telecommunications regulation in the United States by the FCC. As discussed earlier, Director, as Editor of the *Journal of Law & Economics*, often encouraged the publication of articles critical of governmental regulation.

11 Coase indicates that, at the London School of Economics, he "had been responsible for the course on the economics of public utilities" which led him to study British broadcasting (Coase 1988 at 248).

12 An interesting paper discussing Coase's earlier work on this subject is David M. Levy and Sandra J. Peart 2014.

13 Coase 1988 at 248–249.

14 Coase recounts that Stigler and Milton Friedman had been at Stanford the year preceding his and knew of his work (Kitch 1983 at 222).

15 I do not know, but I do not believe that Director had any serious concern about the free speech issues involved.

Coase's opposition to the BBC's telecommunications monopoly in Britain made him an obvious candidate to write on U.S. telecommunications regulation. This assignment, however, would lead to a revolutionary advance in law and economics on account of the brilliance of Ronald Coase.

Regulation of telecommunications in the United States by the FCC was substantially different than regulation in Britain by the BBC. First, in the United States, there was no monopoly; there were many different broadcasters. But, in the United States, because of this fact, there was a peculiar form of regulation based on the claim of potential interference among radio and, separately, television wave lengths, a problem not faced with the BBC monopoly. In theUnited States, the FCC was given authority to allocate wave lengths to radio and television stations in order to prevent one station from interfering with another. The FCC conducted this process through extensive hearings, both to evaluate the petition of an aspiring new entrant and to renew an existing limited-term license.

Second, there is a strong free speech tradition in the United States; the BBC's suppression of Churchill's opinions could not have occurred. Nevertheless, the FCC had promulgated rules such as the "fairness standard" (requiring fair treatment of some opposing differences in view), and requiring each broadcasting station to demonstrate, at the time of renewal of its license, that it had operated "in the public interest." Among other features, this standard had been interpreted to empower direct suppression of some forms of speech: at the time, by communists, pornographers, and some civil rights activists, the principal grounds motivating political liberals in the United States to oppose governmental regulation, again one of the reasons Director brought in Coase.

In the paper Coase wrote for the *Journal of Law & Economics*, "The Federal Communications Commission" (Coase 1959), Coase alludes to these issues, but raises a more fundamental question: what is the need for government regulation of telecommunications at all? The principal justification was that government regulation of telecommunications was necessary, given a limited telecommunications spectrum, to prevent one broadcaster from interfering with another where the separate wavelengths they possessed overlapped over some range, creating interference which would reduce the aggregate value of the telecommunications spectrum.

Coase argued that the problem of potential interference did not require government ownership and allocation of frequencies, but only the definition of property rights to portions of the spectrum to private entities in the market.[16] Government ownership and subsequent allocation of frequencies (without appropriate pricing) was necessarily ineffective. The market would allocate those rights to maximize spectrum value.

16 Coase had not made this argument in his 1950 book *British Broadcasting*, but again, there was no competition in telecommunications in Britain.

Here is Coase's view about the government and the relative superiority of the market with respect to the allocation of spectrum from "The Federal Communications Commission." I quote this passage extensively because it shows Coase's basic analysis, his evolving view of how governments operate, and the role of the market in potentially correcting governmental decisions. Coase described his approach as a

> 'novel theory' (novel with Adam Smith) [which] is, of course, that the allocation of resources should be determined by the forces of the market rather than as a result of government decisions. Quite apart from misallocations which are the result of political pressures, an administrative agency which attempts to perform the function normally carried out by the pricing mechanism operates under two handicaps. First of all, it lacks the precise monetary measure of benefit and cost provided by the market. Second, it cannot, by the nature of things, be in possession of all the relevant information possessed by the managers of every business which uses or might use radio frequencies, to say nothing of the preferences of consumers for the various goods and services in the production of which radio frequencies could be used. In fact, lengthy investigations are required to uncover part of this information, and decisions of the Federal Communications Commission emerge only after long delays, often extending to years. [fn.: It is inevitable that the industry will know more than the Commission.] To simplify the task, the … Commission adopts arbitrary rules. For example, it allocates certain ranges of frequencies (and only these) to certain specified uses. … Commissioner Lee explained: I am finding it increasingly difficult to explain why a steel company, desperate for additional frequency space cannot use a frequency assigned, let us say, to the forest service in an area where there are no trees. [n. excluded.].
>
> This discussion should not be taken to imply that an administrative allocation of resources is inevitably worse than an allocation by means of the price mechanism. [Here back to the analysis of "The Nature of the Firm."] The operation of a market is not itself costless, and, if the costs of operating the market exceeded the costs of running the agency by a sufficiently large amount, we might be willing to acquiesce in the malallocation of resources resulting from the agency's lack of knowledge, inflexibility, and exposure to political pressure. But in the United States few people think that this would be so in most industries, and there is nothing about the broadcasting industry which would lead us to believe that the allocation of frequencies constitutes an exceptional case.
>
> *(Coase 1959 at 18–19)*

Coase would go on in this article to develop his revolutionary idea of the reciprocal nature of the causation of harm. The broadcasting context was important to the development of this idea. If two radio or television stations possess frequency rights that cause interference, which station is to blame? The causation of harm is reciprocal. Coase also explained that it did not matter whether the government initially made mistaken allocations of frequencies since, with a clear definition of property rights to the spectrum, the market would later correct whatever the government did. Both of these ideas would become central to Coase's argument in his seminal paper "The Problem of Social Cost."

Coase presented his FCC paper at Chicago elaborating his ideas about the reciprocal nature of harm and the role of the market, given a definition of property rights, in correcting mistaken governmental decisions. He would later expand and generalize this analysis in "The Problem of Social Cost." All are familiar with the revolutionary impact of the "Social Cost" paper on the way the legal world thinks about the effects of liability rules. It is sometimes forgotten that the ideas of the article were revolutionary at the time to Chicago economists as well. It is a favorite story in Chicago circles of the intellectual revolution that occurred at Chicago on the evening following the workshop at which Coase presented his FCC paper.[17] Apparently, at the workshop and the evening thereafter, Coase had moved beyond broadcasting, and had generalized the ideas, asserting that they exposed the deep theoretical flaw in the work of the prominent British welfare economist Arthur Pigou, whose career had been based on the idea that the government could improve social welfare by levying taxes or offering subsidies to firms whose activities imposed costs on others—by internalizing those costs. In the case of broadcasting, Pigou might have argued that one of the broadcasters causing interference harmed the other and so should be penalized by a tax or liability judgment to correct the harm. Coase had apparently generalized the idea, showing that, if market transactions were allowed, liability rules would have no effect.

Director invited Coase to his home after dinner, along with central figures of the Chicago School: Milton Friedman, Stigler, Reuben Kessel, Gregg Louis, Arnold Harberger, Lloyd Mintz, John McGee, and others. As I have heard the story from Coase,[18] the evening was characterized by Ronald presenting his view and Milton Friedman "knocking [him] down"; Ronald again presenting his view, and Friedman again knocking him down, and so it continued. Ronald noted only that toward the end of the evening Friedman was knocking him down at a somewhat slower pace. Stigler tells that by the close, no one any longer supported Pigou, Ronald's arguments were undamaged, but Stigler himself was unpersuaded. Stigler has described the evening several times as the most exciting intellectual experience of his life.[19]

17 Coase recounts that many at Chicago believed that his discussion of property rights in the FCC article was mistaken. He has said that the agreed to give the workshop at Chicago "to discuss my error with them" (Coase 1993a at 249–250).

18 For a slightly different version of the story, see Kitch 1983 at 106–107. I also heard the story from Stigler.

19 Kitch 1983 at 221–222.

Prior to "The Problem of Social Cost," it was widely believed that legal rules, especially assignments of liability, had actual effects. In an example given earlier, if a landowner possessing a stream is held liable to a downstream landowner for the damages suffered by the downstream landowner from an artificial flooding of the stream, the artificial flooding would stop. The legal system through the liability rule would affect whether flooding occurred, thus ending the externality imposed by the upstream on the downstream landowner. Coase showed based on economic analysis that this was not true, and that whether the artificial flooding continued or not depended not at all on the legal rule for or against the upstream landowner, but on transaction costs. This was a revolutionary insight and extended the impact of economic theory beyond antitrust and regulation to all of law.

Coase's "The Problem of Social Cost" establishes what has been called the Coase Theorem: in the absence of transaction costs, the assignment of liability will have no effect on the allocation of resources.[20] Coase's proof of the point draws on illustrations from English common-law tort and property law cases and from examples presented by A.C. Pigou, the prominent English welfare economist whom Coase was refuting. An initial example looked at a dispute between a cattle owner and a neighboring farmer whose crops were damaged by wandering cattle. Coase showed that whether the cattle owner was held liable for the crop damage caused by raising wandering cattle or was held immune leaving the losses on the farmer, the allocation of resources as between cattle and crops would be the same. He provided similar examples later in the paper of steam railroads emitting sparks destroying crops (authorized railroads were immune from liability for such losses under English law); of an owner of rabbits (selling them for fur and meats) whose rabbits wandered from the owner's property, causing damage to neighboring property; and of a doctor who built a sitting room adjacent to a separate confectioner whose kitchen machinery made it difficult for the doctor to examine patients. In each case, the assignment of liability or immunity from liability had no effect on the number of steam railroads run, the size of the crop, the number of rabbits, or the amount of confectionery produced or medical consultations conducted.

These results occurred in each of these cases because, after a court ruled one way or another in the damage action or after the Parliament enacted a statute defining rights (such as the immunity for steam railroads for damage from sparks), the parties affected could and would renegotiate their obligations in order to maximize total joint output to their mutual benefit. The liability rules or statutory entitlements had no effect because, whatever they were, the parties through the market would reallocate relative obligations in order to achieve maximal joint welfare.

20 Coase himself never defined such a theorem—it was apparently coined by Stigler—but its later popular development is consistent with Coase's analysis.

This was a generalization of Coase's point in "The Federal Communications Commission" that there was no need for government regulation of telecommunications interference. Given a defined set of property rights, the parties could determine the appropriate allocation of resources to maximize joint and societal welfare.

The caveat to the conclusion, however, and of substantial significance, was the existence of transaction costs: the costs of dealing in the market, which Coase had identified as an important economic factor in "The Nature of the Firm." The costs of entering transactions to reallocate property use after a liability decision or a statutory enactment may be too high to make a reallocation beneficial. Thus, the actual economic effect of a liability rule or statute depended not on the content of the rule or of the law, but on whether the magnitude of transaction costs prevented a subsequent market reallocation.

This was a revolutionary insight which, when fully appreciated, shocked the legal community. Several scholars attempted to refute the point, all unsuccessfully. From the beginning of legal education, scholars had studied legal rules and laws presuming that they effected behavior in the society. As the functional approach to law began to develop, scholars debated these effects and promoted the achievement of one set of effects, rather than another. This was the purpose of legal training and education and experience, constituting the life work of the lawyer or academic. Coase's "The Problem of Social Cost" showed that this extensive study and these debates were largely irrelevant. The most important determinant of the allocation of societal resources, given the market, was the magnitude of transaction costs.

I have discussed the initial Chicago School resistance to Coase's idea. Of course, it is not surprising that academics, brilliant in their own fields, might be resistant to an idea that shows that most legal rules and statutes will have no effect, subject to transaction costs. But why would the Chicagoans so strongly resist Coase's argument?

"The Problem of Social Cost" offers an analytical framework for considering the effect of a legal rule which Coase presents in three separate ways.[21] Coase's first approach is to argue that the concept of causation in law or in ordinary language has no meaning in economics. In economic terms, both the injurer and the injured may be said to have been in a position to have caused an accident. This point has become familiar, although there remains modern resistance.[22] One cannot believe, however, that it was this insight that the Chicagoans

21 This description of the article derives from conversations with George Fletcher.

22 In a widely accepted article on the effects of strict liability and negligence standards, Shavell 1980 presents a model in which, contrary to Coase, some proportion of the accident rate can be directly attributed to the activity of the injurer; a different proportion to the activity of the victim. In a concluding section Shavell criticizes Coase's causal relativism approach directly. Shavell's distinction between unilateral harm and bilateral harm ignores Coase.

resisted.[23] The Chicago School is not known as a defender of ordinary language. Indeed, one would think that the group would embrace the approach as offering a new avenue for economic imperialism.

Coase's second approach is to demonstrate the lack of effect of a legal rule on the allocation of resources where transaction costs are zero. This demonstration, of course, is accepted as the theorem of the paper and, indeed, is accepted so broadly that it is difficult today to convince a student that it ever qualified as an insight. Again, although one cannot fully imagine the intellectual context of the time, one would not think that the Chicago School would object to this approach. One distinctive view of the Chicago School in economic thought is its assumption of nearly perfectly operating markets in all commodities.[24] The zero transaction cost assumption reveals the existence, hitherto unappreciated, of markets that deny the effect of legal rules. Coase might be said, by this idea, to have out-Chicagoed Chicago, but the Chicagoans are not likely to have contested his effort.

Coase regarded his third approach as the most central to the paper; it echoes themes that run through many other of his articles. It was Coase's third approach, I believe, that was contested by the Chicago School because it represents a deep conflict over empirical presumptions about the world. We tend now to regard "The Problem of Social Cost" as having been fully accepted by the academy; it is the most frequently cited article in both legal and economic journals. The third and most central approach of the article, however, is now completely ignored.

The Chicago School view of the world has prevailed. The sharp difference between Coase's approach and the main-line Chicago approach was suppressed in part because of difficulties of measurement and in part because Posner's later reinterpretation and application of Coase paints over the conflict.

Coase presents the approach by two arithmetical examples in contexts in which transactions costs are sufficiently high to prevent bargaining around liability rules. We all remember the introduction of positive transaction costs as illustrative of how liability rules can affect the allocation of resources. In these forgotten examples, however, Coase goes further and shows that where transaction costs are positive, an initially "optimal" assignment of liability can lead to suboptimal resource use and, in reverse, a seemingly "suboptimal" assignment can lead to optimal resource use.

23 In Coase's Lecture upon receiving the Nobel Prize, he suggests, among other passages, that the Chicago economists were upset about his discussion of *Sturges v. Bridgeman* (the confectioner versus doctor case mentioned above), which Coase uses as an illustration of reciprocal causation (Coase 2014 at 168–170). I am skeptical of this remembrance of his discussion of the meeting, since Coase had demonstrated the point convincingly in "The Federal Communications Commission." I regret not ever pressing Coase, Stigler, or other Chicagoans who attended the meeting on this subject.

24 Reder 1982 at 11–13.

The example is drawn so that resource use is optimal where the railroad, emitting sparks, runs one train per day and the farmer plants some initial crop level. In the first example, the railroad is not liable for crop damage. Because the private gain to the railroad from a second train is greater than its costs, the railroad runs a second train. The second train, however, causes additional crop damage greater than the incremental value of the train, so that total incremental social product declines.[25]

In the second example, the railroad is made liable for crop damage, possibly in response to the crop damage in the first example. (The discussion is confusing even at this date.) Here, the farmer increases cultivation leading the railroad to shut down, reducing total social product. In the example, the court makes an optimal marginal decision, but given the total product of the activities, reduces the value of resources rather than enhancing them. Coase stresses the now-familiar Coasian lesson that it is necessary for an economist to consider the total social product of alternative liability regimes (Coase 1988 at 138–142).

Coase's emphasis of the divergence between marginal changes in social product and total changes in social product conflicts with the general viewpoint of the Chicago School. The Chicago approach in most contexts is to presume that the world is at a position that very closely approximates total equilibrium. Thus, welfare implications can be deduced from the study of marginal changes alone.[26] Coase, however, criticizes the excessive focus on marginal effects instead of total effects, identifying this approach with the Pigovian tradition.[27] Perhaps it was Coase's insistence on the importance of evaluating the total, rather than the marginal, social product that made the Chicagoans reluctant to accept his approach. Occasionally, one observes Chicagoans today slipping into the Pigovian language of internalization.

Why is there a divergence between marginal changes and total changes in social product in the Coase examples? Coase imagines extremely blunt legal rules. Either the railroad is liable for all damage or for no damage. Furthermore, the examples incorporate the behavioral assumption that the non-liable party will act to maximize the payments that the liable party must make, and there is substantial technological range introduced in which this suboptimal behavior may take place. These assumptions, however, transform the nature of the appropriate marginal decision. Given these assumptions, the ultimate liability choice is not between one train or two trains per day, as Coase initially suggests, but between no railroads or no crops. Thus, the actual marginal product decision is a total product decision. The discrepancy in result arises because the court (or the Pigovian) mistakenly believes that the choice between one and two trains

25 Total incremental social product is the difference between total product from the use of resources as a railroad and in alternative uses.

26 Reder 1982.

27 Of course, Coase also criticizes Pigou for his simple urging of the internalization of costs, which ignores the relative marginal costs of prevention altogether.

per day is all that is at issue. Coase's example, thus, presents something of a second-best problem.

However familiar the article is today, the political dimension of Coase's analysis and how his article fits within the Chicago School tradition are often unappreciated. The article is remembered as vastly changing our understanding of the effects of legal rules. But I do not believe that it was drafted with that ambition in mind and the article does not remotely pursue the implications for the effects of tort law or even more generally of property law, though his examples come from property law cases.[28] That work was later accomplished by Harold Demsetz, Richard Posner, and others. Coase's article, instead, was directed at attacking Pigou and Pigou's purported demonstration that government, including the courts, could and should intervene in multiple markets to correct what we now call externalities. The point of the article was to show that Pigou's analysis of correcting externalities was unsupportable.

The political or ideological dimension of the Coase Theorem is often ignored. To Coase, the implication of the proposition that "In the absence of transaction costs, the assignment of liability will have no effect on the allocation of resources" is that courts and the government can do no good by interfering in markets. Courts and the government are fooling themselves by attempting to improve upon market outcomes and should stay out. Perhaps, though this is an implicit point, if government action can somehow reduce transaction costs, that may enhance welfare. But Coase's ambition was to deflate arguments for more intrusive government, not—as it happened—to revolutionize our understanding of the operation of the legal system. To show Coase's academic program, it is not often remembered that the academic project to which Coase turned after "The Problem of Social Cost" was not the extension of the Coase Theorem to the analysis of legal rules, but an attack on one of the last major institutional vestiges of governmental socialism in Western societies, the post office, similar to his earlier criticism on monopoly grounds of the BBC.[29]

At the time, the character of Coase's insight seemed and, to some extent, still seems today as an indicia of extraordinary genius. I remember thinking then, having been earlier trained to the idea that legal rules had effects, how could a person generate such a counterintuitive idea, and discussing the question with Dick Posner and, later, Harold Demsetz, among others. The extraordinary nature of the intuition led many to look back at Coase's earlier writings to attempt to discover possible precursors of the idea. Important in this respect was Coase's "The Nature of the Firm" (Coase 1937). As discussed, Coase identifies the transaction costs of using the price mechanism, in contrast to direct ordering

28 Coase said in his Nobel Prize Lecture that he had no general aim to transform microeconomics (Coase 1991 at 142).

29 Coase 1961. Several years later, as a student, I was able to write a paper which Coase had encouraged Dick Posner to write but which Posner, less interested in Coase's program to attack state intervention in the market, handed off to me, his research assistant on the project (Priest 1975).

within a firm. Many, including the Nobel Prize Committee, have regarded Coase's early focus on transaction cost reduction as an explanation for the creation of a firm as at one with the recognition of the importance of transaction costs in determining the effects of legal rules.

I am skeptical of this explanation for two reasons. First, Coase's work after "The Nature of the Firm" did not generally focus on the implications of transaction costs. Second, there is a more direct source of the analysis in the "Problem of Social Cost", consistent more broadly with Coase's and Director's beliefs. Again, the principal ambition of "The Problem of Social Cost" was to show that Pigou's rationalization of broad governmental, including judicial, intervention in the marketplace was both foolish and ineffectual. The Coase Theorem follows directly from a belief system that sees market transactions as inherently superior to government interventions. If one sees a problem, an externality, that government intervention is attempting to solve, but believes deeply that the market will solve the problem more effectively, the analysis of "The Problem of Social Cost" becomes more apparent. Market transactions can serve to solve problems among conflicting property uses that governmental interventions cannot hope to equal. The Coase Theorem fits squarely within the Chicago School tradition that views markets as superior means of allocating resources and that, conversely, views governmental interventions as generally lacking analytical support and harmful in effect.

Richard Posner has described Coase's article as the first to enunciate the theory that common-law rules are efficient (Posner 1972a; Posner 1981). In earlier sections of "The Problem of Social Cost" (Coase 1960 at 19), Coase does mention that courts seem more aware of causal relativism than did Pigou, and he proposes that individual judicial decisions may have enhanced the value of resources (Coase 1988 at 122–126). Coase's arithmetical examples, however, belie a serious acceptance of the theory of efficient rules. In Richard Posner's legal world, as shall be explained, one would not have observed excessive investment by the farmer or railroad, because the liability rules would be more precisely defined to maximize welfare. Thus, the farmer could not have doubled his crops without exposing himself to liability (assumption of risk, contributory negligence), though the railroad is generally held liable for crop damage. In Coase's examples, on the other hand, the courts are unable to fine-tune legal rules. The suboptimal marginal decision becomes optimal because courts cannot do any better (Coase 1960 at 43). Coase, perhaps anticipating the Posnerian alternative, emphasizes that economists should ignore the description of ideal worlds and take social institutions as they find them.

If Coase hoped to inspire the comparison of total social products rather than marginal social products, he of course was disappointed. Calabresi's *Cost of Accidents* comes perhaps closest to the objective, although the work of both later-Calabresi and Posner focuses relentlessly on marginal comparisons alone. The presumption of the Chicago School has dominated after all. Of course, the comparison of the total social products of different legal regimes is a formidable task, and I know of no successful example in the law and economics literature. One of the great virtues of the Chicago School focus on marginal changes is that the focus allows the derivation of nearly-unambiguous implications. I am not certain that the Coasian method would do so. Coase may accept this point. He sums up his discussion of the evaluation of the effects of legal rules with the otherwise mysterious invocation of Frank Knight, the famous Chicago economist who resisted the simplifications of the Chicago School:[30] "As Frank H. Knight has so often emphasized," Coase concludes, "problems of welfare economics must ultimately dissolve into a study of aesthetics and morals" (Coase 1960 at 43).

It required more than a decade for the academic community to settle upon the meaning of "The Problem of Social Cost." As late as 1972, Harold Demsetz was still writing articles explaining Coase's point—and they are important articles (Demsetz 1972a, 1972b). There was another flurry of definition a decade later.[31]

Coase's ideas in "The Federal Communications Commission" and "The Problem of Social Cost" vastly expanded the scope of law and economics. The field was no longer limited to the study of industrial organization, affected by government policies through antitrust and regulatory law. The field of law and economics now extended to all of law, including seemingly backwater topics such as torts, contracts, and property. Especially, "The Problem of Social Cost" showed that long-expected effects of legal rules were uncertain or, more precisely, had to be analyzed more carefully according to these economic ideas. It also showed that the role of government was more limited than was generally accepted and that the market played the more important, perhaps the definitive, role in determining the allocation of resources.

In fact, there is a radical political nature to "The Problem of Social Cost" that has not been sufficiently emphasized. Its ideas represent an extraordinary devaluation of the importance of governmental decisions with respect to the allocation of resources versus those decisions made in the marketplace. Note that the grounds for Coase's devaluation of governmental decisions to allocate resources is quite different from Hayek's and von Mises's. Hayek's and von Mises's point is that there will always be more aggregate information in the market than available to any government decision-maker, and thus that market decisions will be preferable. Coase, I believe, would accept this point as a precondition (again, to my knowledge, without ever relying on Hayek or von Mises). Coase in "The Problem of Social Cost," however, argues that the accumulation of knowledge in the market as to how resources can be most effectively allocated will always be superior to governmental decisions and will be implemented despite government decisions. In this respect, Coase, importantly, does not accept the road to serfdom. Coase believes that bargaining in the marketplace where market transactions are allowed to operate will evade that road.

30 Reder 1982 at 6.
31 Aivazian & Callen 1981; Coase 1988.

As an example of Coase's radical view about the significance of markets in overturning political decisions and the primacy of market decisions over any political allocation: after one class, in which Mr. Coase had made this point strongly, I pursued him after class and trailing him down[32] asked him just outside his office (this is a paraphrase), Mr. Coase, certainly the President of the United States has political influence over the allocation of resources? Mr. Coase wheeled and replied to me (no paraphrase), "The influence of the President of the United States is $200,000." $200,000 was then the salary of the President, by which Coase meant that the President could influence the economy only to the extent of the President's personal purchasing power in the marketplace.

32 In my experience, Mr. Coase was not particularly interested in interactions with students and would, typically, bolt from the classroom at the end of class.

6

CALABRESI AND THE ECONOMIC FRAMEWORK OF *THE COSTS OF ACCIDENTS*

James' work, discussed in Chapter 4, building on Douglas, importantly advanced commitment to the analysis that the law should be viewed and treated functionally, though James' single functional goal was to expand risk distribution. James' protégé, my colleague Guido Calabresi (Figure 6.1), shifted the form of James' analysis dramatically, placing it into an explicit economic framework.

Calabresi's addition here was highly innovative and a quantum leap in terms of economic sophistication from James and Douglas. Calabresi's initial article, "Some Thoughts on Risk Distribution and the Law of Torts" (Calabresi 1961), was in fact published almost simultaneously to Coase's "The Problem of Social Cost," although dated later,[1] and it took law and economics to a new level. The paper did not provide the conceptual innovation of Coase, but it attempted to apply economic analysis seriously to the issue that dominated James' work: risk distribution. Calabresi wrote several other articles later and engaged in a spirited debate with Blum and Kalven, discussed in Chapter 4, over automobile compensation plans.[2] In all of these articles, Calabresi emphasized the importance of economic analysis to the then-understanding of the effects of legal rules.

Calabresi, perhaps more than Coase and certainly more than Posner, had economic training.[3] He majored in economics at Yale College, though the Yale economics department at the time was subject to great criticism, most

1 Coase's article was dated 1960. *The Journal of Law & Economics*, in its early years, experienced publication delays, so that Coase's article, appearing in the 1960 issue of the *Journal*, actually came out in early 1961. See Kitch 1983 at 221.

2 See Chapter 4, *supra*.

3 Much of the information about Calabresi's early training derives from conversations with Norman Silber, who is writing a forthcoming biography of Calabresi.

FIGURE 6.1 Guido Calabresi (c. 1960s)
Photo courtesy of Yale Law School

prominently by William F. Buckley, who described it as doctrinaire. The then Yale President, A. Whitney Griswold, perhaps in response to this criticism, brought in substantial new blood, including James Tobin, a subsequent Nobel laureate, and William Fellner, with both of whom Calabresi studied. Calabresi was awarded a Rhodes scholarship and studied with John Hicks and Lawrence Klein, both Nobel laureates, in England. He returned to the United States, entered Yale Law School, where he taught an undergraduate economics section, subsequently clerked on the Supreme Court for Justice Black, and afterwards began teaching at Yale.

As mentioned, Calabresi published several important articles early in his career. His initial article, modestly entitled "Some Thoughts on Risk Distribution and the Law of Torts," introduced economic analysis into the field. He generalized his approach in 1970 in his justly famous book *The Costs of Accidents*. Here, Calabresi more formally put the consideration of the functional effects of legal rules into a direct economic framework. Coase had not done so, and never did so, because Coase's broader analysis was the market determination of the allocation of resources. Calabresi did not generally address the operation of the market—to the extent he did, he thought, in sharp opposition to Coase, that the market was ineffective, although most of his discussion addresses accident law where transaction costs are likely to be high.

Calabresi begins the heart of his book with the stirring statement: "I take it as axiomatic that the principal function of accident law is to reduce the sum of the costs of accidents and the costs of avoiding accidents" (Calabresi 1970 at 26).[4] Calabresi defines three sets of costs:

1. "Primary costs" are the direct costs of accidents in terms of lost lives, hospital expenses, pain and suffering, time away from work, rehabilitation, and property loss: costs reimbursed through tort law damages.
2. "Secondary costs" are defined as the costs of failing to adequately compensate victims; the costs of providing for victims "after the accident" (Calabresi 1970 at 27). There is some mystery to this definition. If primary costs are calculated appropriately, there would be no failure of adequate compensation, including costs suffered "after the accident," since the common law nominally awards full rehabilitation costs as well as past and future pain and suffering. As later expounded in the book, Calabresi is terming "secondary costs" as the consideration of risk and wealth distribution policies. This follows, though puts an economic cast on, James' primary emphasis.
3. "Tertiary costs" are the costs of administering the system.

Calabresi here provides an economic framework for the analysis of the effects of legal rules and moves what was simply a functional approach into an economic approach. He defines three types of costs, costs according to standard economic analysis to be weighed against the benefits of the legal rule. Although, as I shall explain, Calabresi does not really define an economic cost/benefit equilibrium, his analytical framework provides a substantial advance to the economic analysis of law.

Modern law and economics scholars would fully accept the goal of minimizing what Calabresi calls primary and tertiary costs—accident losses and administrative costs[5]—at least net of benefits. But there is no careful evaluation of costs versus benefits in Calabresi, except to recognize the general benefits of driving and of walking. A driver hitting a pedestrian is Calabresi's principal example of an accident.

The central feature of the Calabresian analysis is his treatment of what he calls "secondary" costs. Secondary costs are the most important in the Calabresian view—they are described in detail first and most extensively. As mentioned, Calabresi defines them as the costs of failing adequately to compensate victims. According to Calabresi, our views about the allocation of these losses are implicated with our views about the distribution of wealth and of risks across the

4 Actually, the book begins with an evaluation of accident compensation plan proposals which, though relevant to the dominant academic debate at the time, underemphasizes the book's novel conceptual power.

5 Law and economics scholars today generally ignore Calabresi's tertiary—administrative—costs, on the acknowledgement that the system of administering the law is not determined by the differential content of legal rules. Of course, the achievement of efficiencies in administering the system would be an economic benefit.

society (Calabresi 1970 at 39–54).[6] Calabresi claims that it is clear that the society—as a society—desires to spread risks and distribute losses over some broad section of the population. There are theoretical justifications for such an objective: a belief either in the diminishing marginal utility of money, although Calabresi admits that this proposition is discredited (however much he continues to emphasize it) (Calabresi 1970 at 39–40); that individuals cannot properly evaluate risks; that the costs of spreading risks are higher to individuals than to corporate enterprises; or that individuals will not properly spread risks because they do not know what is good for them or because they are judgment-proof (Calabresi 1970 at 39–52, 55–60).

Theory aside, according to Calabresi, there is evidence that society wants to spread risks broadly. First, the institution of the progressive income tax shows a desire to take from the "deep pocket" for the support of social ends (Calabresi 1970 at 40).[7] Second, although private insurance serves to spread losses to some extent, there is evidence that society views spreading by private insurance as inadequate. Modern decisions in the law of consumer contracts and products liability which deny effect to disclaimers of liability or exculpatory clauses require sellers to provide insurance that consumers did not voluntarily purchase. These decisions, Calabresi argues, can only be explained as fulfilling a societal (as opposed to a private market) desire to distribute losses (Calabresi 1970 at 50–54). Assigned risk pools express the same desire (Calabresi 1970 at 62–63). Thus, both in terms of theory and evidence, there are strong reasons to suggest that the reduction of secondary costs by loss spreading (beyond that of private insurance or the fault system) is a societal goal equal in importance to the reduction of primary and tertiary costs. In a style of argument invoked continuously by Calabresi he claims that no one must accept all of these reasons for loss spreading, but no one can reject them all (Calabresi 1970 at 64).

It is evident that Calabresi's secondary costs relate to James', and to Calabresi's following James', belief that distributional values must play an important role in accident law. This was central to James' agenda. It is equally central to Calabresi's: the title of his first article was "Some Thoughts on Risk Distribution and the Law of Torts." Calabresi attempts to integrate these distributional values into his economic model by denominating them as "costs," supposedly costs, along with primary and tertiary costs, true economic costs, to be optimized against benefits.

Here, Calabresi departs from standard economic analysis; certainly from modern economic analysis, but from the older standard economic analysis as well: I know of no treatment of welfare economics which treats wealth

6 Calabresi frequently conflates risk distribution policies with wealth redistribution policies.

7 An example of the conflation of risk distribution and wealth redistribution. This conflation occurs because Calabresi's chief—though not only—defense of risk distribution is on the grounds of the diminishing marginal utility of money.

distributional preferences as "costs" to be weighed against, say, the costs of injuries or the costs of preventing injuries. Calabresi's treatment here is supportive of James' insistence that the liability system promote risk redistribution, though he takes it a step further by claiming that these distributional preferences are "costs" in the economic sense. It is not obvious how illuminating the "cost" terminology is. Calabresi does not really aspire to reduce wealth distributional preferences as one would aspire to reduce costs but, at best, to reallocate them according to different preferences.

According to Calabresi, there are two methods for reducing the sum of these three types of costs: general deterrence and specific deterrence. General deterrence, through the market, places accident costs on the party that causes[8] the accident, in the same way that the price system places the cost of a resource on the person who consumes the resource. General deterrence will reduce accident costs because the prospect of bearing these costs will encourage individuals to engage in behavior less likely to cause accidents.[9] According to Calabresi, like other market processes, general deterrence is inadequate itself to optimally reduce costs because it fails to take into account either (1) the distribution of wealth in society (and thus may aggravate a maldistribution of wealth); (2) that some individuals are judgment-proof and indifferent to the potential imposition of accident costs; and (3) other market failures such as monopoly or second-best misallocations (Calabresi 1970 at 78–88). According to Calabresi, "To describe a world of perfect general deterrence is to refute its possibility" (Calabresi 1970 at 88).

Specific deterrence supplements general deterrence by addressing particular activities directly. Specific deterrence may penalize activities such as drunk driving or speeding (which Calabresi describes as sinful) or may exempt activities from the general deterrent if the activity is regarded as especially worthy; Calabresi (then young) suggests, as an example, driving by aged men (Calabresi 1970 at 295).

Specific deterrent methods are justified because a mixed system of general and specific deterrence can reach a broader set of activities than a system of general deterrence alone (Calabresi 1970 at 180–181).[10] Furthermore, specific deterrence repairs the failures of general deterrence by allowing wealth distribution to be more comprehensively considered and by providing for the expression of moral judgments of the society (*id.* at 96–105). Calabresi emphasizes the distinction between the private decision-based general deterrence and the collective decision-based specific deterrence (*id.* at 96, 106–107). Again, he argues that not

8 Here Calabresi, perhaps in response to Coase, hedges his definition of the word "cause." Calabresi will later devote substantial attention to the meaning of this term. See text at Chapter 8, *infra*.

9 Calabresi focuses principally on the effect of damage judgments on the level of activity.

10 Calabresi also adds, "Since in practice we will never want pure general deterrence, it is not worthwhile discussing at length which forum and method are most likely to accomplish it" (Calabresi 1970 at 161).

everyone would accept all of the various bases for specific deterrence, "but virtually everyone would accept at least one" (*id.* at 96).

There is a long history of discussion, especially in the criminal law field, of what is called "general deterrence" and "specific deterrence." The distinction in criminal law is between a prohibition of a general nature, addressed to the population at large, versus a specific prohibition of a particular person, whose criminal activities are sought to be deterred.

Calabresi invokes these legal terms, "general" and "specific" deterrence, in a far different way: the distinction and, in particular, the term "specific deterrence" is transformed into an additional means to achieve the welfare distributional ambitions that he and James expressed earlier, though this is now a substantial expansion of James. Calabresi's terminological transformation becomes a further tool toward inculcating welfare distribution into accident law.

This distillation of Calabresi's analysis into three sets of costs and the distinction between what he calls general and specific deterrence capture the basis of his ideas, but grossly understate the complexity of his treatment in his effort comprehensively to both explain and, at the same time, criticize all of accident law. Calabresi is able to explain every feature of modern accident law according to these concepts. But Calabresi also uses the concepts to open for criticism every feature that fails to achieve what he thinks the society wants in terms of appropriate wealth distribution. To illustrate the complexity of Calabresi's analysis, in an early passage in *The Costs of Accidents* he explains

> The question of who should bear the costs of a particular accident, or of all accidents, is to be decided on the basis of the goals we wish accident law to accomplish. Thus it is a policy question whether accident costs should be (1) borne by particular victims; (2) paid on a one-to-one basis by those who injure a particular victim; (3) borne by those broad categories of people who are likely to be victims; (4) paid by those broad categories of people who are likely to be injurers; (5) paid by those who in some sense violate our moral codes (in some sense are at fault) according to the degree of their wrongdoing, whether or not they are involved in accidents; (6) paid by those who in some actuarial sense are most likely to violate our moral codes; (7) paid from the general coffers of the state or by particular industry groups in accordance with criteria (such as wealth) that may be totally unrelated to accident involvement; or (8) paid by some combination of these methods. … [I]n considering the bases of accident law, there are virtually no limits on how we can allocate or divide the costs of accidents.
>
> *(Calabresi 1970 at 22–23)*

To Calabresi, all mechanisms of public policy are available to deal with the auto accident problem (or, by extension, with any other societal problem).

How does our current system of accident law measure up according to this framework? According to Calabresi, it fails miserably to achieve our societal goals. The accident system appears designed to achieve some confused mixture of all of the goals of accident law by various and often contradictory means. The system allocates accident costs on the basis of fault, but the concept of individual fault is anachronistic.[11] Today, individuals are unable to take all risks fully into account in their driving or walking behavior. The fault system completely ignores the existence of private insurance which eliminates incentives for individuals to take greater care (*id.* at 269), although insurance may affect the level of individual activities. The fault system's mistaken focus on personal shortcomings neglects any attempt to determine that class of injurer or injured (corresponding to insurance classes) that is the best accident avoider or best briber (of the other party) or best insurer (the concept of best avoider, best briber, and the like, was an innovation of Calabresi) (Calabresi 1970 at 244–256). In addition, the fault system places all accident costs on one of the parties to the accident, rather than creating dual incentives for optimal joint avoidance (*id.* at 259–263).

James emphasized that the practices of liability insurance carriers would more importantly determine the real world substance of tort law than the rules of tort law themselves. Calabresi follows this lead. This is not an unimportant point, but its practical effect should be put in context. Calabresi explains that the detailed examination of the circumstances of an accident as would happen in a trial—did Driver A signal or not?—is not taken into account in insurance companies' setting of insurance premium rates and, so, represents a wasted accumulation of information. James and Calabresi argue that these particularistic judgments by courts and juries collect irrelevant information and so increase the costs of the accident system.

Neither James nor Calabresi presents empirical data to support this assertion and the range of its importance is questionable. Insurance companies do not set rates according to traffic signaling. But the generation by the liability system of a verdict against a 70-year-old man because he did not signal versus leaving the loss on a 30-year-old woman because the question was not pursued can be important in the establishment of differential insurance rates. James and Calabresi argued that the private liability insurance system overrides the tort system at great additional cost. But this is not true. If insurance companies, by aggregating and segregating risks, can reduce the effective costs of accidents, that is a societal benefit and similar in effect to reducing administrative costs generally. Neither James nor Calabresi carefully understands the operation and effect of modern liability insurance.

Most importantly, according to Calabresi, the fault system ignores secondary costs. Like the market, the system inadequately considers wealth distribution, the

11 See, in particular, Calabresi's discussion of the advantages of a worker compensation regime (Calabresi 1970 at 245–246).

values of tapping the deep pocket (*id.* at 245–279) and the general societal advantage from shifting risks more broadly (*id.* at 251–252, 278). Of course, the system ignores other market imperfections (monopoly, second-best misallocations) as well (*id.* at 278). In addition, the fault system is grossly more costly to administer than it need be.

How should the system be reformed? Calabresi abjures specific proposals (*id.* at 312), although his preferences are clear enough. Certainly, the case-by-case system of trial by jury would be abandoned for most accident cases (*id.* at 302). The private insurance market would be more closely regulated (*id.* at 311–312); more extensive specific deterrent incentives would be introduced: damages, for example, "could be buttressed by an array of non-insurable fines, penalties and taxes" and "[c]onversely, subsidies could be given to those categories [of activities that] ... were collectively deemed especially desirable" (*id.* at 312) (more examples here of Calabresi's "specific deterrence"); pain and suffering damages would be eliminated;[12] a compensation fund might be created. Calabresi concludes optimistically that these details can be worked out; what he has shown is that a mixed system of general and specific deterrence could be adopted that "does all the things we want in the way of accident cost reduction better than the fault system" (*id.* at 312).

Calabresi wrote many articles and books after *The Costs of Accidents*. Some of them were related to his basic analysis of accident law (Calabresi 1971). Expanding the approach beyond traffic accidents, he proposed (with Hirschoff) a standard for strict products liability (Calabresi and Hirschoff 1972). He addressed more carefully the issue of causation in tort law, though again arguing that the issue could be interpreted to achieve any of the values he had espoused (Calabresi 1975b, 1975c). He did not, however, seek to apply his analysis broadly to other areas of the law.

Calabresi reacted negatively to Coase's "Problem of Social Cost." It was published, as mentioned above, almost simultaneously to Calabresi's "Some Thoughts on Risk Distribution." Calabresi's response might be expected: Coase's point was that the market would reallocate resources regardless of the liability rules that Calabresi had so painstakingly tried to justify, though Coase never dealt with automobile accidents. Calabresi published an article in 1968 attempting to limit the scope of the Coase Theorem (Calabresi 1968). The article basically claims that there are wealth effects from the assignment of liability to one party or the other: that is, that the confectioner or the doctor will comparatively benefit pecuniarily from winning the property rights dispute. Coase did not disagree with this point and admitted that he had neglected it in "The Problem of Social Cost." The empirical relevance of the point for accidents and even for property disputes is probably negligible.

12 Calabresi believes that the particular individual is the best insurer of non-economic loss (Calabresi 1970 at 223).

Calabresi also argued in this article, anticipating his subsequent arguments in *The Costs of Accidents*, that it was simply an empirical question what type of rule or legal structure would lead to optimal resource allocation:

> The question then becomes: Is this [optimal resource allocation] accomplished most accurately and most cheaply by structural rules (like antitrust laws), by liability rules, by taxation and governmental spending, by letting the market have free play, or by some combination of these?
>
> *(Calabresi 1968 at 69)*

He answered that courts and lawyers needed to make guesses as to what actions would lead to the optimal results, but then asserted—similar to his insistence on the primacy of what he would call "secondary costs" in *The Costs of Accidents*—that "[a]ction in uncertain cases is more likely to be justified if goals *other* than resource allocation (like proper income distribution) are served by the action" (*id.*). Calabresi later wrote a famous paper on causation that argued, in the typical Calabresian style, that to achieve "appropriate" societal ends, anything can be claimed to be the cause of a harm, applying the analytical structure of *The Costs of Accidents* to the issue (Calabresi 1975b).[13]

Later, perhaps working through more seriously the implications of the Coase Theorem, Calabresi published an article with A. Douglas Melamed distinguishing three separate types of legal rules: property rules, liability rules, and inalienability rules (Calabresi and Melamed 1972).[14] It remains an important article. Arguably, Coase's analysis dealt with property rules and liability rules. But the Coase Theorem did not address inalienability rules: rules that prohibit market transactions to overcome them. Coase had certainly considered such rules: the regulatory allocations of frequencies addressed in "The Federal Communications Commission" article were examples (Coase 1988 at 117). Certainly, the argument of Coase's paper was that the FCC should get out of the business of setting such regulations, allowing the market to allocate radio and TV frequencies. And perhaps that was the hope of Coase's "The Federal Communications Commission." But Calabresi and Melamed expanded the point and demonstrated in the legal system far more of what they called "inalienability" rules than ever discussed by Coase.

Calabresi's analysis, however, set law and economics on a bold new course. Coase had shown, through the employment of economic analysis, that economic forces—the operation of the market—would triumph over the determination of legal rules. Calabresi, separately, provided an economic framework for James' functional view of the law, though greatly expanded it, focusing on the

13 See also Calabresi, "You Can Call It Thucydides or You Can Call It Mustard Plaster, But It's All Proximate Cause Just the Same!" 91 *Yale Law Journal* 1 (1981).

14 This distinction was anticipated in Calabresi's 1968 article at 69.

economic effects of specific legal rules. He emphasized rules he called "specific deterrence" which aimed to effect wealth distribution, as he emphasized rules affecting risk and wealth distribution more generally. As we shall see, modern law and economics has not generally followed Calabresi's emphasis of risk and wealth redistribution. But the economic framework into which Calabresi placed the analysis of the law had extraordinary influence toward acceptance of economic analysis of law.

7

LAW AND ECONOMICS MADE DOMINANT

Richard A. Posner and *Economic Analysis of Law*

Richard Posner expanded the application of the economic framework far beyond the realm of auto accidents—Calabresi's subject—to all of law, most importantly to all of private law—torts, contracts, and property—and demonstrated the importance of economic analysis to public law topics as well. Posner forced the legal academy not only to acknowledge law and economics, but to come to grips with it. Calabresi's *Costs of Accidents*, however brilliant, had not had this effect. Though Calabresi's analytical framework could have been generalized to other areas of law, he did not do so, nor did others, and Calabresi's focus in the book on auto accidents seemed to limit its scope. Of course, that Calabresi's book was so complicated, discussing infinite variations of rules, also made it difficult to make clearly operational.

In contrast, Richard Posner (Figure 7.1) compelled attention to law and economics (subsequently aided by his gifted colleague William Landes; Figure 7.2) by claiming that a simple concept of economics—the concept of efficiency—explained the content of private law much more effectively than any alternative explanation put forth by any previous legal academic. Posner's endeavor demonstrated the importance of economic analysis of law and rocketed the field of law and economics to the center of legal analysis and, because of the force of his sustained endeavor, to the dominant center.

Posner was an unlikely economist,[1] even more an unlikely Chicago School economist. His parents were immigrants: his mother from Austria, his father from Romania (Domnarski at 9). Neither had money when they arrived. Posner's father was a member of the Communist Party (*id.*), and his mother,

1 A point made in a fine biography: William Domnarski, *Richard Posner*, at 1 (2016). Many of the details of Posner's early life are taken from Domnarski.

FIGURE 7.1 Richard A. Posner (c. 1970s)
Photo courtesy of the University of Chicago Law School

possibly but not clearly a communist, surely was a strong union organizer (*id.* at 14). It is an oft-repeated story (which Posner also told me) that, as a boy, Posner's mother took his toys from him and gave them to the Rosenberg children (the children of the atomic spies for the Soviet Union who were executed). Posner told Domnarski that he was too old for the toys anyway (*id.*). Posner's parents were industrious and became affluent. Posner was later raised in Scarsdale, New York (*id.* at 27).

Posner was brilliant throughout his education. He attended Yale College and was an English major. He was chosen as a Scholar of the House, an honor given to ten students (of a class of roughly 1,000), granting them the senior year without classes to write an extensive dissertation. Posner wrote on the poetry of William Butler Yeats. One of Posner's earlier law school colleagues told me that Posner had completed the dissertation in August before the school year began. Posner then attended Harvard Law School, was President of the Harvard Law Review, and graduated first in his class. Next, Posner clerked for Justice Brennan on the Supreme Court, and has described his political views as "a political liberal [assisting] Brennan with enthusiasm, indeed with relish" (*id.* at 41).

This would change. Posner is attributed as writing Brennan's antitrust opinion in the *Philadelphia National Bank* case, which employs economic reasoning with respect to a prospective bank merger. After the clerkship, he served as an assistant to Philip Elman, a Commissioner of the Federal Trade Commission, and there purportedly wrote many opinions including the Commission's antitrust opinion in *Proctor & Gamble*. Posner then became general counsel of a Presidential Task Force on Communications Policy, where he worked with the economist Leland Johnson (Domnarski at 52). In this position, he wrote a memo recommending that AT&T be broken up, which reached the desk of President Lyndon Johnson, who personally suppressed it (*id.*).

Posner then took an academic job at Stanford Law School, though he is said to have told the Dean, Bayless Manning, that he did not see himself as writing academic articles (*id.* at 53). This proved to be a huge misestimation. Posner jumped into writing. He immediately wrote provocative articles on economic regulation and on tacit collusion under the Sherman Act (Posner 1968a, 1968b). At Stanford, Posner was substantially influenced by Aaron Director, who had retired there from Chicago (Domnarski at 53). Posner cites Director as the source of many of the ideas of his regulation and collusion articles. Posner also met George Stigler, who spent winter terms at Stanford.

Director was closely involved in Posner's move the next year, 1969, to the University of Chicago Law School. Apparently, Director called the Dean of the Chicago Law School, urging him to hire Posner, and convinced Posner to move there (*id.* at 56–57). At Chicago, Posner subsequently taught seminars with Director, who occasionally returned (*id.* at 60). Domnarski describes Posner as committed to economic analysis of law upon joining the Chicago faculty.

One of Posner's early articles at Chicago was a review of Calabresi's *The Costs of Accidents* (Posner 1970). This review presages much of Posner's later important work in law and economics.

Although ultimately critical of Calabresi's specific proposals, Posner strongly praises Calabresi's general application of economic analysis to the legal problem of auto accidents. Posner states that Calabresi's work "mark[s] a new direction in legal scholarship" (*id.* at 636). More effusively, Posner explains

> The utilization of this systematic procedure to bring elementary but profound insights of economic theory to bear on the accident question proves a powerful forensic and analytical machine with which Calabresi easily sweeps rival approaches, employing more conventional legal analytic methods, from the board. He demonstrates that these methods overlook important consequences of different accident control schemes, proceed on no coherent theory, and provide little useful guidance to policy makers; and that an approach grounded in the procedures and theorems of economics offers greater promise.
>
> (id. *at 644)*

Posner concludes, nonetheless, that however impressive Calabresi's economic approach, his conclusion that the fault system must be replaced is based on unverified assertions uninformed by facts. "[T]he alleged shortcomings of the [fault system must be] verified by empirical research" (*id.* at 644–647).

Posner, in 1972, would found the *Journal of Legal Studies*, initially dedicated to publishing empirical studies of the legal system. Indeed, Posner's criticism of the absence of facts in Calabresi and Posner's curative proposals for the future appear in retrospect as a program for the forthcoming *Journal of Legal Studies*.

After criticizing Calabresi's lack of empirical research, Posner proposes three empirical studies that he believes "would cast considerable light on ... whether the fault system is better at reducing the net costs of accidents than alternative systems." The first is a cross-jurisdictional study of accident rates in states with different accident law rules; the second is a comparison of whether changes in accident technology affected the costs of accident avoidance and subsequent legal rules. These would be difficult studies, and in the nearly five decades since Posner's review and the founding of the *Journal of Legal Studies*, no one has completed either one.

Posner's third proposed study, however, was ultimately taken up by Posner himself in applying economic analysis to law. The third proposal is to "ask how many of the doctrines of accident law currently in force can be deduced from the premise that the purpose of such law is to reduce the (net) costs of accidents" (*id.* at 647–648).

Posner leapt into this third method of evaluating the economic effects of the law almost immediately. In 1971, he published an article, "Killing or Wounding to Protect a Property Interest," in the *Journal of Law & Economics* (Posner 1971a), in which he sought to determine how the common-law rules on this subject corresponded to an economic approach. The issue addressed is the liability of landowners for injuries caused by weaponry they had installed—such as spring guns—to repel trespassers seeking to steal property, often plant products—break-ins of tulip and watermelon gardens are examples. It is an obscure issue in tort law[2] and, to my knowledge, the article drew little notice. Posner finds that the case law "seems broadly consistent with an economic approach" (Posner 1971a at 218).

Posner's style in the article is vastly different than that he would later adopt to propel law and economics to the center of legal scholarship. Much like a standard law review article, Posner devotes the first seventeen pages of the article to a criticism of the relevant provisions of the Restatement of Torts and to a conceptual discussion of the costs and benefits of various methods of preventing theft by trespassers, such as building higher fences, using less harmful forms of weaponry, hiring a watchman, and the like.

2 Posner claims, in contrast, that the issue is "curiously central" to tort law, invoking cases dealing with the destruction of trespassing domestic animals and the "private necessity" cases such as *Ploof v. Putnam*, 51 Vt. 471, 71 A. 188 (1908) (Posner 1971a).

He then devotes only four and a half pages to a discussion of the case law and finds that most cases confirm his earlier evaluation of the costs versus benefits of property protection.[3] Posner concludes that

> [b]y utilizing the approach to tort questions sketched here, legal scholarship has an opportunity to effect a drastic and necessary simplification of doctrine [meaning the reform of the Restatement] and to place the analysis of tort law on a more functional basis.
>
> (id. *at 227)*

As mentioned, Posner's "Killing and Wounding," to my knowledge, attracted little attention. Posner's next effort to show the economic content of common-law rules, in contrast, did. Indeed, the article stamped law and economics as the dominant explanatory theory of the law. In the next year, 1972, Posner published "A Theory of Negligence" in the first issue of his *Journal of Legal Studies*.[4] Here, Posner vastly expanded the scope of his approach by claiming that all but one of the hundreds of the rules of the negligence standard, the most central standard of tort law, were efficient.[5] He made the point explicit: "Perhaps, then, the dominant function of the fault system is to generate rules of liability that, if followed, will bring about, at least approximately, the efficient—the cost justified—level of accidents and safety" (Posner 1971a at 33).

Posner, in this article, challenges all tort scholars, asserting that the simple economic concept of efficiency—the optimization of costs and benefits—explains common-law rules in every area of tort law. This article goes far beyond Posner's earlier discussion of the rules addressing spring guns in cottages and gardens. According to Posner, of the rules of tort law governing every accident context, all but one are defined to achieve economic efficiency.

The style of Posner's presentation changes dramatically from "Killing and Wounding." The "Negligence" article does not begin with a thoughtful rumination of costs and benefits. Posner briefly explains competing explanations, declares his far different point, and then immediately presents the case law, doctrine by doctrine, explaining why each rule is efficient.

For purposes of the study, Posner drew a sample of 1,528 American federal and state appellate court accident law decisions, comprising each opinion issued in the first quarter of 1875, 1885, 1895, and 1905, a period he calls "the classic flowering

3 Posner notes, however, given the substantial state legislative regulation of the field that "[t]he economic calculus seems much less clearly at work in the legislative product" (*id.* at 223).

4 1972b. Domnarski reports that Coase told Posner that he was willing to publish his articles, such as "Killing and Wounding," but that it would be better if Posner started his own journal, presaging their differences, described more fully in Chapter 8.

5 The one exception was the lack of liability of a corporation for the negligence of its doctors (*id.* at 70).

of the negligence concept."[6] He supplemented the appellate sample by reviewing trial cases involving railroad and street railway accidents in Cook and DuPage Counties, Illinois which include Chicago and a rural adjoining area.[7]

Note the scope of Posner's effort. At the time, a law review article studying twenty to thirty cases may have been the norm; an article studying fifty cases would have been exceptional. Posner studied 1,528 cases.

The cases address disparate issues. For each one of them, however, Posner finds that the rule of law applied generates the efficient outcome. To illustrate the analysis, Posner finds efficient:

1. the distinction between the duty of due care in basic negligence and the duty of the highest practicable care, owed by common carriers (railroads and tramways), as a likely approximation of what would be agreed upon by the parties to a contract of carriage (*id.* at 38);
2. the exception to the due care duty with respect to trespassers, because such a duty would interfere with rights of exclusive property possession (*id.*);
3. the rule that compliance with custom is not a defense, in order to create incentives for improvements in accident prevention (*id.* at 39);
4. the normal disallowance of punitive damages, because most victims of negligence can identify their injurers so common-law compensatory damages have no need to be increased and, thus, constitute the economically appropriate deterrent (*id.* at 41);
5. the doctrine of proximate cause, because no precautions are needed against accidents that occur rarely (*id.* at 42);
6. the doctrine of *respondeat superior,* because a company is in the best position to decide how much to invest in preventing workers from being careless (*id.* at 43);
7. the lack of application of *respondeat superior* to families, because children are harder to control than workers (*id.*);
8. the fellow-servant rule, in order to give employees an incentive to report careless co-workers, called by Posner "a powerful instrument for industrial safety" (*id.* at 44);
9. the rules of contributory negligence and assumption of risk generally and in the employment context, to create incentives for victims for precaution (*id.* at 40, 45–46).

Posner also finds common-law measures of damages for injury and death to be efficient (*id.* at 46–48).

In many areas, state and federal legislatures had preempted common-law rules of negligence. This was true generally with the acceptance by courts that an

6 *Id.* at 34. Posner estimates that his sample constitutes one thirtieth of all appellate accident cases during the period (*id.*).

7 *Id.* at 36. The review of trial cases adds little to the point.

accident occurring in the context of a violation of a statute constituted negligence per se. But it was also true more specifically, especially in the employment context, with the detailed regulation of safety procedures, especially during the period examined, for railroads, and the adoption of worker compensation statutes that abrogated the fellow-servant and assumption-of-risk rules. Posner's commitment to common-law negligence as efficiency makes him critical of this legislation. "It would appear that the purpose of the legislation was to improve the lot of the risk-neutral or risk-averse worker at the expense of risk-preferring workers (and of consumers)," contradictory to efficiency (*id.* at 71–72).

Note the differences here between Posner and Calabresi. First, Calabresi's analysis of primary, secondary, and tertiary costs with what he calls "specific deterrence" allows for infinite variation in the definition of accident rules, depending upon what societal objective is desired. Posner, in contrast, claims that a single standard controls: efficiency. Thus, if the costs and benefits of a rule or behavior could be measured precisely, there would be one rule, and only one rule, that achieved that end. Not so to Calabresi. Calabresi's "secondary costs" reflect the preferences of the citizenry as to appropriate risk/wealth redistribution. The rules that those preferences may generate were infinite in possibility. Second, Calabresi easily explains statutory safety regulation (as a form of specific deterrence) and the subsidization of the risk-averse by the risk-preferring as reflecting what he calls "secondary costs." Posner disdains subsidization because it does not achieve economic efficiency.

Although "A Theory of Negligence" dealt only with the private law subject of tort law, its import was far broader. Posner's findings were dazzling. The seemingly scientific character of the study deriving from the sample of 1,528 cases meant that no legal scholar could honestly ignore the findings. This effect extended not only to torts and private law scholars, but to legal scholars in all fields. Posner seemed to have discovered something about the operation of the legal system that had not been recognized before. The centrality of the economic concept of efficiency over the broad range of tort law—indeed, the almost unanimity of efficiency found in the cases—made obvious the centrality of law and economics.

Posner's next major endeavor cemented the centrality of law and economics for all of law. In 1973, he published *Economic Analysis of Law*, a textbook that demonstrated how all of law—now both public and private law—could be usefully analyzed through the lens of economics (Posner 1973b).

Part I of the book addresses common-law areas: property, contracts, torts, and crimes.[8] In these chapters, Posner does not extensively review common-law case

8 *Id.* at Chapters 2–5. Posner states that crimes resemble torts, except that with respect to crimes, courts "do not compare the value to the contestants of the right in question" (*id.* at 67–68). Many crimes, such as theft and rape, are punished because the underlying action contravenes what might have been a market transaction (*id.*). The book has little else to say about the content of substantive criminal law. In a much later chapter, Posner explains how the determination of criminal penalties

law, but explains how the basic doctrines of each field seem to derive from the concept of economic efficiency.[9] Posner concludes these chapters by claiming that there is "an implicit economic logic of the common law …; [T]he common law exhibits a deep unity that is economic in character" (Posner 1973b at 98). Posner does not propose an explanatory theory as to how this came about, although he relates it to the adversarial method of common-law adjudication:

> [T]he character of common law litigation forces a confrontation with economic issues. The typical common law case involves a dispute between two parties over which one should bear a loss. In searching for a reasonably objective and impartial standard, as the traditions of the bench require him to do, the judge can hardly fail to consider whether the loss was the product of wasteful, uneconomical resource use. In a culture of scarcity, this is an urgent, an inescapable question. And at least an approximation to the answer is in most cases reasonably accessible to intuition and common sense.
>
> (id. *at 99, footnote omitted)*

By this he means efficiency.

In the textbook, Posner extends the application of economics to legal issues to include much of public law, including direct economic fields: monopoly, antitrust law, taxation, and effects on poverty; constitutional issues: federalism, racial discrimination, and free speech; and legal process issues: civil procedure, judicial administration, and criminal punishment. In these chapters, Posner does not claim that the law is efficient; in fact, he is generally critical of many doctrines in these areas because they seem to reflect distributional or political judgments instead of the economic concept of efficiency.[10] Posner, nevertheless, expands the scope of law and economics by showing how economic analysis can helpfully illuminate paths to choose in the context of general areas of public policy.

Economic Analysis of Law extended and consolidated law and economics to importantly explain the doctrines of all of the common law and to criticize on economic grounds much of public law. The book established the relevance of law and economics—and, in particular, Posner's law and economics—to all of law.

corresponds to an economic analysis of the problem (*id.* at Chapter 25). Posner would expand his explanation of substantive criminal law in, 1985 and in later editions of the book, *see*, *Economic Analysis of Law* at Chapter 7 (9th ed.; 2014).

9 There is some attention to case law. In the Property chapter, Posner discusses some of the spring gun cases reviewed in "A Theory of Negligence"; in the Contracts chapter, there is some discussion of individual cases, all demonstrating efficiency; the Torts chapter, of course, heavily relies on, though does not duplicate, the case law discussion in "A Theory of Negligence."

10 Note that Posner does not cite any of the public choice literature with respect to this point.

Posner cites Calabresi sparingly,[11] but does not address Calabresi's approach or conclusions in any detail. Posner does not need to. Posner had presented not only a theory alternative to Calabresi's, but a dominant alternative theory both because he could explain the case law in detail—as in "Theory of Negligence"—in a way Calabresi never attempted and because Posner had extended economic analysis to all of law, which went far beyond Calabresi's *Costs of Accidents*.

Economic Analysis of Law was widely reviewed, and by many prominent academics, but his efficiency theory of the common law generated substantial criticism.[12] Many legal scholars complained that Posner had ignored a wide range of dominant social values by giving attention to efficiency alone, and that Posner's wealth maximization definition of efficiency ignored distributional values. Perhaps the most telling argument was that Posner disregarded the values that judges themselves had identified in their opinions as the basis for their decisions. It was also argued that Posner's "tacit economic logic" of the common law was supported only by Posner's interpretation of the relevant costs and benefits, which were vaguely specified. Further, Posner was criticized for failing to identify a plausible cause by which the common law developed this economic logic.

Many of these criticisms had substantial merit. Much of the discussion of the efficiency-of-the-law in *Economic Analysis* is at a quite general level. Take Posner's more specific claims in "A Theory of Negligence." For example, what is the basis for concluding that passengers on common carriers prefer and are willing to pay for actions meeting "the highest standard of care" (Posner 1971b at 38) rather than a negligence standard attended by lower fares? Similarly, what is the basis for the conclusion that children are harder to control in terms of harm-causing activities than employees, justifying on economic grounds different standards of *respondeat superior*? (Posner 1971b at 43).

Posner, jumping at the bit, responded to these various criticisms in a 1975 article, "The Economic Approach to Law."[13] His defense was chiefly methodological: All scientific theories are abstractions. The only valid criticism of a theory (such as efficiency-of-the-law) is the presentation of a superior theory.

Perhaps seeing that "A Theory of Negligence" and *Economic Analysis of Law* had not been totally convincing, and recognizing that this methodological defense would not be ultimately convincing, Posner began a serious program, lasting for nearly a decade and a half, writing individual papers to further convince the academy that his efficiency-of-the-law theory should be dominant. In many of these articles, he was aided by his colleague, William Landes; sometimes, with others. In retrospect, it constitutes an extraordinary academic endeavor.

11 *Id.* at 84 (Calabresi's attack on the negligence system); *id.* at 88n (Calabresi's discussion of no-fault proposals); *id.* at 29n, 68n (the discussion of inalienability in Calabresi & Melamed 1972).

12 Among others, see Buchanan 1974; Diamond 1974; Leff 1974; Tullock 1974 (basically complaining that Posner had only incidentally cited Tullock's *The Logic of the Law*, a much weaker book).

13 Posner 1975. Posner admits in the article that "[m]any of these criticisms are not yet in print" (*id.* at 772).

The program consisted of three different avenues of argument. As in "The Theory of Negligence," Posner and often Posner and Landes surveyed individual areas of law to determine whether their legal rules were consistent with the efficiency hypothesis. First, they specifically chose legal areas that might seem adverse to the economic approach. Thus, in 1977, Posner published an article on the law of gratuitous promises, promises made not on the basis of market transactions, which he described as "at first glance, resistant to economics" (Posner 1977 at 424). He found the rules of this area of law generally consistent with his efficiency approach (*id.*). In an article published in 1980, Posner and Landes studied the law of joint and multiple tortfeasors, what they called "a particularly challenging setting" (Landes & Posner 1980 at 517). Again, on the whole, the rules of this field approximated economic efficiency (*id.* at 517, 530). In 1981, Landes and Posner published "An Economic Theory of Intentional Torts," emphasizing that "[i]ntent is not a normal part of an economist's vocabulary and does not appear to correspond to any concept in economics" (Landes & Posner 1981 at 127). They found that economics could give content to the concepts of the field and could reconcile seeming dichotomies in the law (*id.* at 145). In 1985, Posner published "An Economic Theory of the Criminal Law," explaining that "concepts that dominate substantive criminal law such as attempt, conspiracy, entrapment, insanity, and premeditation seem alien to an economist's way of thinking about problems" (Posner 1985 at 1194), showing, however, that the "substantive doctrines of criminal law, as of the common law in general, ... can indeed be shown to promote efficiency" (*id.*).

The second avenue of argument was to survey—in the manner of "A Theory of Negligence"—individual areas of law not carefully discussed in Posner's *Economic Analysis* to examine whether the rules corresponded to the efficiency hypothesis. In 1977, Posner (with Andrew Rosenfeld) published an article on cases related to the impossibility doctrine in contract law (Posner & Rosenfield 1977). They found "an implied economic logic," "an internal economic logic" to these rules (*id.* at 84, 118). In 1978, Posner published an article, "The Right to Privacy," finding the rules of that area of law "broadly consistent with the economics of the problem" (Posner 1978 at 409, 421). In 1978, Landes and Posner published an article on the law of rescue (Posner 1978), finding again that "the major doctrines and case outcomes are shaped by a concern for promoting economic efficiency" (*id.* at 85).

And so it went. In 1985, Landes and Posner extended the analysis to products liability law (Landes & Posner 1985). The support for the efficiency-of-the-law theory continued to mount. Finally, over this same period, Landes and Posner would contribute other articles, not principally claiming the efficiency-of-the-law, but applying economics to new areas of legal practice, demonstrating the effectiveness of economic analysis to understanding the operation of the legal system. Landes' 1971 article "An Economic Analysis of the Courts" was important in this regard, as was Posner's 1973 article "An Economic Approach to Legal Procedure and Judicial Administration" (Posner 1973a). Of course, several

FIGURE 7.2 William Landes (c. 1980s)
Photo courtesy of the University of Chicago Law School

of their earlier articles had shown the utility of economic analysis in clarifying obscure areas of the law.[14] Posner also continued adding to *Economic Analysis of Law* in subsequent editions. The book is currently in its ninth edition (2014).

Posner's encyclopedic application of economic analysis to all of law was aided—and, perhaps in part, inspired—by Gary Becker's application of economic analysis to areas of human endeavor far beyond business and industry. Becker's Ph.D dissertation addressed economic forces affecting racial discrimination (Becker 1971). He wrote an important paper on criminal punishment (Becker 1968), which surely informed and reinforced Posner's broad application of economic analysis. Becker, of course, extended the approach in later works (Becker 1976; Posner 1981). Becker and Posner were colleagues and later jointly published an entertaining blog.

In the late 1970s, Posner attempted to bolster his efficiency-of-the-law theory by defining a coherent moral philosophy, to be ascribed to judges, of maximizing the wealth of the society (Posner 1979, 1980a).[15] His efforts were a response to the criticisms of, among others, Frank Michelman, who argued that wealth maximization was too unappealing a value to ascribe to common-law judges (Michelman 1979). Posner

14 See, in particular, Posner and Rosenfield 1977 at 100 (courts have not clarified the principles of law in this area); Posner 1978 at 84 (although treated in different areas of law—torts, contracts, admiralty—the issues raise different examples of a single problem).

15 Posner later rewrote these articles for a book, *The Economics of Justice* (1981).

carefully distinguished the principle of wealth maximization from utilitarianism. But his argument for the principle drew substantial criticism from several distinguished philosophers.[16] Posner later abandoned the point.

Posner's efficiency-of-the-law theory may not have been initially accepted, but it is important to distinguish between the acceptance of a theory and its intellectual importance. At the time that Calabresi's *Costs of Accidents* and Posner's *Economic Analysis of Law* were published, I would imagine that nearly every legal scholar to whom the competing positions were explained[17] would have found Calabresi's approach the more congenial and plausible. Nevertheless, Posner's theory had much greater influence than Calabresi's both on those conducting subsequent research in the field and those obliged to consider that research. The efficiency-of-the-law literature is voluminous, though in substantial part by Posner and Landes. In contrast, other than Calabresi's *Costs of Accidents*, there are few, if any, scholars who have seriously pursued Calabresi's definitions of costs, especially of the influence of secondary costs (risk and wealth distribution).[18]

Why was Posner's approach received so differently than Calabresi's? Why did Posner's theory give birth to as many zealous enemies as it did to zealous disciples? One possible, but I believe incomplete, explanation is the simplicity of Posner's theory. Compare Posner's unidimensional theory of common-law rules to Calabresi's infinitely dimensional theory.

A stronger explanation is the adoption by Posner of a positive scientific approach in contrast to the openly normative approach of Calabresi. In some respects, this contrast is overstated. It is misleading to describe *Economic Analysis of Law* as solely positive in nature. In the first chapters of the book, Posner purports to prove that the central principle of the common law is efficiency. Yet, the prescriptive nature of the demonstration is obvious. If, for some reason, common-law adjudication leads inexorably to efficient rules, it would be counterproductive and, finally, futile for a court to adopt an inefficient rule. Indeed, if an institution as central to our culture as the common law embraces efficiency, why should not our policies in non-common-law areas be defined to achieve efficiency as well? In the first edition of the book, Posner devotes only the first ninety-three pages to common-law efficiency; the 292 that follow show how the central theme of the common law can be applied to statutory and regulatory fields. And the unanimity in the demonstration of common-law efficiency added to the force of Posner's efficiency criticisms in his discussion of the various areas of public law.

Calabresi's *Costs of Accidents* also incorporates substantial positive elements. As discussed, Calabresi infers societal values from existing social institutions, just as Posner infers efficiency from existing legal rules. This positive approach could

16 For example, Dworkin 1980; Kronman 1980; Weinrib 1980. Posner responded to these criticisms in Posner 1981, Chapter 4.

17 I am skeptical (from my own experience initially and, again, for purposes of this book) that many scholars read Calabresi's *Costs of Accidents* thoroughly because of its extreme complexity.

18 The Calabresi–Melamed article (1972), in contrast, has been deeply influential.

have been elaborated by Calabresi by carefully reviewing the rules of various legal areas to show how they are consistent with Calabresian values. But Calabresi did not do so. His later work is relentlessly normative. In his 1972 article with Hirschoff, he applies the cost concepts from *The Costs of Accidents* to propose a new rule of strict liability for product defect cases (Calabresi & Hirschoff 1972). Similarly, in his 1975 causation article, Calabresi shows how the analytic framework of *The Costs of Accidents* can be applied to achieve any societal goal using the legal concept of "causation" (Calabresi 1975b).

The scientific patina of the Posner approach, however, allowed legal scholars to support Posner's conclusions while abjuring value judgments. This characteristic of Posner accounts for both the numbers of fervent critics and the equally fervent support that Posner received. It also contributed substantially to the rise of law and economics.

Posner's unidimensional scientific theory allows a scholar to discuss the legal system in a sophisticated way without having to defend any value judgment implicit in the discussion. All scientific discussions abstract from value judgments at some level. Posner's single-value theory, however, possesses a tremendous advantage over a Calabresian multiple-value theory in this respect. A unidimensional theory is less subject to the criticism that it is tautologous. Posner's single-value theory is much more resistant to interpretive criticism than Calabresi's. The estimation of costs and benefits describes a fairly restricted area for dispute. Compare a test of a Calabresian hypothesis that some rule of law is optimal as measured by the sum of primary and tertiary costs adjusted by societal views about risk allocation and wealth distribution. However scientific the commitments of the discussants, it would be impossible to avoid debate over the importance of the various competing values.

The ability to abstain from value judgments was a tremendous benefit to the adherents of Posner's theory. It became possible to discuss efficiency seriously without ever immersing in the endless discussions about how important economic efficiency ought to be. One could disclaim personal adherence to efficiency as a value, but invoke the necessity of understanding the common law. The Posnerite could be a Galileo swearing loyalty to the Church while pointing at sunspots. Indeed, the discovery that Chicago School economics was the basis of the common law gave new and heretofore unknown general legitimacy to the Chicago School approach in other fields. For exactly the same reason, Posner's apparent scientism enraged his critics.

Calabresi had signaled the importance of economics to the understanding of the law in his study of auto accidents. Posner, taking an entirely different tack, vastly expanded the approach. Posner showed that economic analysis was a significant interpretive tool—perhaps the most significant tool—for all of law. The basic point was established in "A Theory of Negligence" and, shortly thereafter, in *Economic Analysis of Law*. His many subsequent papers, including those written with William Landes, made the conclusion inescapable.

8

COASE, CALABRESI, AND POSNER COMPARED

Coase, Calabresi, and Posner are the central intellectual figures in the rise of modern law and economics. Together, their combined efforts demonstrated the central significance of economic analysis to the understanding both of the effects of the law and of its content. They were justly celebrated as three of the four fundamental founders of the field of law and economics at the first meeting of the American Law and Economics Association in 1991.[1]

The work of the three remains, however, a curious combination. The ideas and approaches of each of these three scholars were widely different. These differences would become manifest in debates among them in succeeding years. Calabresi and Posner debated openly from the start, centrally over Calabresi's commitment to using legal rules to achieve wealth redistribution versus Posner's emphasis on economic efficiency.[2] Having attended some of these debates, they were riveting and certainly enhanced attention to the field. Coase and Posner also had sharply different approaches which would erupt in later years in a vituperous debate, seemingly on methodological issues, discussed below.

Coase was interested in the effects of legal rules on resource allocation in the society. The essence of his analysis was to show that markets could overturn any effect a court thought it might be achieving through a legal ruling, subject to limitations of transaction costs. Coase's analysis showed the central importance of markets, again, limited only by the costs of market transactions.

Calabresi, in contrast, disdained markets, viewing them as ineffectual. Given the constellation of values that Calabresi sought to validate through the law—the chief

1 The fourth was Henry Manne, whose contributions are discussed in Chapter 10.

2 The debate continues. See the discussion of Calabresi's recent book, *The Future of Law and Economics: Essays in Reform and Recollection* (2016), discussed *infra*.

of which were risk distribution and wealth distribution to the poor—Calabresi was right. The market does not directly achieve wealth distribution to the poor, except by providing opportunities to increase skills. The market does provide mechanisms for risk distribution such as insurance, but Calabresi and his mentor, Fleming James, did not understand the economic operation of liability insurance, which is a market response to concerns about risk. Market insurance responds to these concerns by disclaiming risks that are uninsurable—for which there is no economic value from insurance, even if created by the law—and by defining the terms of insurance coverage to create incentives on policyholders to reduce losses.[3]

James and Calabresi never dealt with the fact that there is no benefit from providing "insurance" for uninsurable losses, such as where losses are highly correlated or within the control of the insured. Here, again, their views conflate risk distribution with wealth redistribution. Calabresi and James sought broader distribution of losses without regard to this market alternative, more generally through accident law, though they never sought to define precisely what the wealth redistribution objectives of the society were, understandably, because they could be constantly shifting.

Coase's emphasis on the role of purely market transactions avoids all discussion of societal objectives with respect to risk and wealth redistribution. It could not be further from Calabresi.

Posner's approach acknowledges the existence of markets but, quite in contrast to Coase, greatly devalues markets. Posner understood the point of the Coase Theorem and repeatedly distinguished, in his analysis of individual legal areas, litigation circumstances where transaction costs are likely to be low from those where transaction costs are likely to be high. For example, in contractual disputes, where transaction costs are likely to be low, Posner and Rosenfeld, in their "Impossibility" article, write, "If the rules of contract law are inefficient, the parties … will contract around them. A law of contract not based on efficiency considerations will therefore be largely futile" (Posner & Rosenfield 1977 at 89). Other articles, however, emphasize the importance of economic analysis in contexts of high transaction costs. In their article on products liability, Landes and Posner write, "The explanatory power of economic analysis of law comes from showing why one legal rule is preferable to another given significant transaction costs" (Landes & Posner 1985 at 547). In addition, one of Posner's central explanations of the rules of substantive criminal law is that they serve to prevent the bypassing of market transactions—the prohibition of theft, as an example. (Posner 1985 at 1195).

Despite Posner's recognition of markets, the efficiency-of-the-law approach basically negates any effect markets might have on the allocation of resources, quite to the opposite of Coase. In "The Problem of Social Cost," Coase showed that markets would determine the ultimate allocation of resources in the

3 For a discussion, see Priest 1987 and Priest 2017.

society, regardless of any allocation determined by a court, subject to transaction costs. This is the point of the many farmer–rancher and farmer–railroad examples in the paper. According to Posner's analysis, however, markets are not needed to serve this function. If courts always adopt rules that establish the efficient allocation of resources, subsequent market transactions reallocating resources will not need to occur. Posner's efficiency-of-the-law demonstrations read markets out of the process.

From the start, Posner consistently gave Coase credit for inspiring the efficiency-of-the-law hypothesis. In the first edition of *Economic Analysis of Law*, Posner states, describing what he calls Coase's view, "The common law of nuisance can be understood as an attempt to increase the value of resource use by assigning property rights to those parties to conflicting land uses in whose hands the rights are most valuable" (Posner 1973b at 17).[4] He repeats the point in many subsequent articles (Posner 1975, 1981). The basis for this attribution is a discussion in Coase's "The Problem of Social Cost" that states,

> it is clear from a cursory study that the courts have often recognized the economic implications of their decisions and are aware (as many economists are not) of the reciprocal nature of the problem. Furthermore, from time to time, they take these economic implications into account, along with other factors, in arriving at their decisions (Coase 1988 at 119–20). … The courts do not always refer very clearly to the economic problem posed by the cases brought before them, but it seems probable that in the interpretation of words and phrases like 'reasonable' or 'common or ordinary use' there is some recognition, perhaps largely unconscious and certainly not very explicit, of the economic aspects of the question at issue.
>
> (id. *at 123–24)*

Reading these passages may have put the efficiency-of-the-law idea—and of its tacit character—in Posner's mind. Also probably relevant to Posner's formulation of the idea was Calabresi's discussion in *The Costs of Accidents* of what Calabresi called primary costs (bodily injury and property damages) and tertiary costs (legal administration costs), though Posner totally disregarded Calabresi's discussion of secondary costs (risk and wealth redistribution).

It is obvious, however, that efficiency-of-the-law was not Coase's point. To the opposite, the principal subject of Coase's "The Problem of Social Cost" was how markets would always correct legal rules that failed to allocate resources efficiently. Without court rulings that generated inefficient allocations of resources, Coase would not have had an article.

4 In the most recent edition of the book (9th ed., 2014), Posner states that "Coase intuited that the English law of nuisance had an implicit economic logic" at 36–37.

Despite Posner's generous attribution to Coase, he did not believe that Coase had originated the idea of the efficiency-of-the-law. He remarked in a 2001 interview that his insight "was pretty original" (Domnarski 2016 at 68).

In later years, Coase and Posner had a more significant dispute. Coase at some point distanced himself from the Chicago economics department—Stigler, in particular, possibly Becker; I am not sure.[5] Coase, roughly in 1984, founded a group later to be known as the New Institutional Economics school. The ambition of these scholars was to turn economics from the study of perfect markets and competitive prices to the understanding of how institutions including the firm (deriving from Coase's earliest important article) and governmental institutions operated in the face of differential organizational costs.

In 1993, the group convened a conference to celebrate its tenth anniversary. Introductory remarks by Coase and by my former colleague Oliver Williamson sketched out the achievements of the associated scholars. For some reason, not clear, Richard Posner was also invited to attend and delivered a paper (Posner 1993a) which the organizers of the conference described as "harsh" (Furubotn & Richter 1993).

Posner's published article, which I think must have been toned down from his original paper (Scott 1993), criticized the school and claimed that the supposed New Institutional Economics was merely a restatement in a different vocabulary of ideas from law and economics, in particular deriving from Stigler's article on the economics of information.

Coase and Williamson responded vehemently to the claim that the new school was addressing issues that mainstream Chicago economists had addressed. They claimed that Posner's work and what was then normal law and economics had not identified economic relationships within a firm and within governmental organizations that affected economic outcomes (Williamson 1993; Coase 1993b).

Posner's published paper in the symposium is moderate, perhaps as mentioned because of the effect of commentators. Posner, separately however, published an article in the *Journal of Economic Perspectives* which is scathing of Coase,[6] and quite personal, criticizing Coase's "acid wit" and his "Englishness" (Posner 1993b). Coase and Posner did not leave as friends.

Calabresi would ultimately recognize the brilliance of Coase's idea and, in fact, would claim that he had had the idea of reciprocal causation independently and roughly contemporaneously with Coase. In various publications, and in personal communications, Calabresi has made this argument, stating that his Yale colleague, the economist Ward Bowman, a former Chicagoan in Aaron Director's group, had advised him not to expand it in his initial article, "Some Thoughts on Risk Distribution" (1961).[7]

5 This is the reason that, as a student, I could go out to lunch with Coase and John Peterman twice a week. See, *supra*, Acknowledgements. Coase had abandoned the round table at the Quadrangle Club.

6 Perhaps the material excised from the New Institutional Economics paper.

7 I never asked my late colleague, Ward Bowman, about this, but it seems unusual given that the point is clear in Coase's earlier "Federal Communications" article.

Calabresi has made this claim most recently in 2016 in his book, *The Future of Law and Economics: Essays in Reform and Recollection*, though he adds interesting details in the footnotes to the book.

The point Calabresi made in a footnote in "Some Thoughts on Risk Distribution" was that automobile-pedestrian accidents might be characterized as the consequence either of walking or driving.

> In effect such a result would amount to a decision that automobile accidents are more a true cost of walking and of living generally, than of automobile driving. Actually, they are probably a cost of both.
>
> I have not, in this article, attempted to probe what influences our decision that a particular 'cost' is caused by one activity rather than another. Clearly this is an important question. Indeed, it is the next step in any thorough analysis of risk distribution. At this stage of analysis, however, when we have not yet examined the need and the effect of charging activities with those costs which all would agree they cause, that step seems somewhat far removed.
>
> *(Calabresi 1961 at 499, n. 24)*

In his 2016 book, Calabresi then states that he was unaware of Coase's "Problem of Social Cost" when he wrote his paper. (Again, Coase's "Problem of Social Cost" was published roughly simultaneously to Calabresi's "Some Thoughts on Risk Distribution.")

In the 2016 book, Calabresi admits that

> I did not spell out that causal symmetry as fully as Coase did and most important, Coase's explicit discussion of the internalization of externalities [by which I think he means the effect of markets in overturning inefficient rules] was missing from my piece.
>
> *(Calabresi 2016 at 182, n. 30)*

This is a generous acknowledgement by Calabresi of the importance of Coase's "Problem of Social Cost." In a later footnote in Calabresi 2016 book, he adds further information about the origins of the reciprocal causation idea. Calabresi recounts that, when he was recruited by the University of Chicago Law School in 1960, he

> met with Aaron Director, who asked me if I knew of Coase. I replied that I had read Coase 1959 article, 'The Federal Communications Commission,' but didn't see what it could possibly have to do with 'Some Thoughts.' It wasn't until 'The Problem of Social Cost' appeared soon after that I realized what Director—who had already edited Coase's piece—was referring to.
>
> (id. *at 183, n. 39)*

This, again, is a generous admission by Calabresi,[8] but I think it misses the point of the idea. Clearly, Calabresi had an inkling of the concept of reciprocal causation. How much it derived from his reading of Coase's "Federal Communications Commission" cannot be determined. To be fair to Calabresi, it is surely easier to see reciprocal causation, as Coase did, in the context of interfering radio or television signals than in Calabresi's focus on driver–pedestrian accidents. Reciprocal causation, however, would never have been a major element of Calabresi's discussion of liability rules. Concerned with ultimate effects on risk and wealth redistribution, the concept of reciprocal causation would likely have had no importance to Calabresi's general analysis and, of course, Calabresi believed markets were ineffectual, quite to the contrary of Coase.

There is a deeper similarity, however, between Coase and Calabresi that makes the focus on the idea of reciprocal causation far less important. Neither Coase's analysis nor Calabresi's gives value to the legal concept of causation. Causation, in a legal sense, means nothing to them. For Coase, this is because markets will reallocate resources to maximize joint or common value regardless of any legal attribution of causation. For Calabresi, the objective of legal rules is to minimize the sum of primary, tertiary, and, most importantly, secondary costs (risk and wealth redistribution) again regardless of legal attribution of causation. Conceptually, Coase and Calabresi are united on this point. Richard Posner, instead, is quite the contrast. His analysis relies on legal attributions of causation in order to establish incentives for economically efficient behavior.

As mentioned, following "The Problem of Social Cost" Coase moved on to study and criticize the government monopoly of postal delivery (Coase 1961), and later wrote important papers on the monopoly of durable goods (Coase 1972) and on how seaside lighthouses, seemingly a public good, were supported by markets (Coase 1974); and, of course, promoted the school called the New Institutional Economics (Coase 1998).

Calabresi, after *The Costs of Accidents*, turned his attention to difficult ethical and moral questions (Calabresi 1974a, 1974b, 1975a; Calabresi & Bobbitt 1978), as well as questions about the legal process (Calabresi 1978; 1979; 1982; 1983), all areas highly original, but none closely related to law and economics. Calabresi was appointed a judge on the 2nd Circuit Court of Appeals in 1994.

Posner's relentless publication style continued. He wrote important articles on antitrust law which, along with the writings of Robert Bork, heavily influenced the Supreme Court to adopt a near-Chicago-school approach to the field.[9] He continued to update *Economic Analysis of Law* (now in its ninth edition), but broadened the scope of his work to address topics such as aging (Posner 1995), national security (Posner 2005a, 2005b, 2006a, 2006b, 2007), sexual behavior (Posner 1992), the financial crisis in the United States (Posner 2008), and many

8 From my thirty-seven years as a colleague of Calabresi, he is an infinitely generous man.

9 Discussed in Chapter 9.

others, even after he was appointed a judge on the 7th Circuit Court of Appeals in 1981. His biographer, William Domnarski, interprets Posner's thousands of judicial opinions as continuing his promotion of economic analysis of the law, though I think the interpretation is strained.

Recently, Posner has written on the sources of judicial decision making (though, even more recently, he has resigned his position as judge). Based on his many years on the court, he describes these sources in an almost Jerome Frank interpretation: he describes judicial decisions as based on personal ideas, philosophies, and attitudes of the judge. At a workshop at which he presented these views, I asked him what happened to the tacit economic logic of the law. He responded, "That was a youthful enthusiasm."

9

THE INFLUENCE OF LAW AND ECONOMICS ON REGULATION AND ANTITRUST LAW

Modern law and economics has changed the way scholars, judges, and lawyers view all of law, but the most spectacular successes of the discipline in terms of direct influence on substantive law have occurred in the fields of economic regulation and antitrust law. The deregulation movement of the 1970s is entirely attributable to law and economics scholarship. Federal regulatory institutions, some established in the nineteenth century and others during the New Deal, have been completely eliminated; still others have had their authority limited or diminished. Today, there is little impetus toward expanded economic regulation.[1]

Similarly, since the late 1970s, in antitrust law, the Supreme Court has totally overturned the legal rules it had developed, some since 1911, especially with respect to vertical practices, but extending more broadly. As will be explained, the Supreme Court has directly adopted, and has implemented in many decisions, the Chicago-School consumer welfare standard for evaluating industrial practices. These changes resulted from the ascendance of law and economics and, especially, from the work of Aaron Director, his students, and his journal, the *Journal of Law & Economics*, at the University of Chicago Law School.

Chapter 4 described the University of Chicago Law School's Antitrust Project, led by Aaron Director, which subjected New Deal policies both with respect to industrial regulation and to antitrust law as formulated by the Supreme Court in the 1940s, 1950s, and 1960s to unrelenting scrutiny and criticism. This criticism was both conceptual but also, importantly, empirical.

1 Though there are concerns about the effect of social media on privacy and political interference, different from economic regulation.

The influence on regulation

From the earliest years of the *Journal of Law & Economics*, articles examined the justification for state licensing[2] and the regulation of fishing rights[3] and water rights.[4] Subsequent articles over the years[5] examined the regulation of air[6] and land transport;[7] electric utilities;[8] telecommunications;[9] the provision of natural gas;[10] and many other fields subject to economic regulation, including pharmaceuticals,[11] municipal zoning,[12] meat[13] and milk regulation,[14] dry cleaning,[15] the merchant marine,[16] urban taxis,[17] forestry,[18] liquor,[19] and eyeglasses.[20]

Many of these articles were empirical, but the *Journal* also published articles of substantial theoretical importance such as Stigler and Friedland's analysis of the origins of electric utility regulation,[21] Lerner's discussion of public utility regulation,[22] Bajt's study of the means of production in the Soviet economy,[23] and Harold Demsetz's seminal article, "Why Regulate Utilities?"[24]

These articles were generally critical of government regulation, but also advisory. They brought the economic analysis of regulation to a new intellectual level, beyond that typically provided by the regulators themselves.

These efforts of economic analysis were later joined, after almost a decade and a half, by the founding of the *Bell Journal of Economic and Management Science* in 1970, initially supported by Bell Laboratories, the research division of the national telephone monopoly AT&T, later to become, after the breakup of AT&T, the *Rand Journal*.

2 Moore 1961.
3 Crutchfield 1961.
4 Bagley 1961.
5 I only list here articles published prior to the mid-1970s, when the deregulation movement began.
6 Levine 1969; Davies 1971; Baxter & Altree 1972; Levine 1975.
7 Bowman 1966; Hilton 1966.
8 Stigler & Friedland 1962; Peltzman 1971; Mann 1974.
9 Of course, Coase 1959; but also Levin 1962; Minasian 1964; Peterman 1965; Greenberg 1967; Ohls 1970; Crandall 1971; Comanor & Mitchell 1972; Besen 1974.
10 Gerwig 1962; Dam 1965; Kitch 1968; Dam 1970, 1971; MacAvoy 1971a; Dam 1974.
11 Steele 1962.
12 Crecine, Davis, & Jackson 1967; Siegan 1970 (a highly important article); Stull 1975.
13 Weiss 1964.
14 Kessel 1967; Knutson 1969.
15 Plott 1965.
16 Whitehurst 1965.
17 Kitch, Isaacson, & Kasper 1971; Kitch 1972.
18 Stroup & Baden 1973.
19 Urban & Mancke 1972.
20 Benham 1972.
21 Stigler & Friedland 1962.
22 Lerner 1964.
23 Bajt 1968.
24 Demsetz 1968.

The first Editor of the *Bell Journal* was Paul MacAvoy, who early in his career had served as a Research Associate in Aaron Director's Antitrust Project. The *Bell Journal* published analyses resembling those of the *Journal of Law & Economics* though somewhat more technocratic, with less of a market preference. Articles in the *Bell Journal*, however, similarly advanced the economic analysis of regulatory policy. The *Bell Journal* published several important papers on regulatory theory, in particular Stigler's "The Theory of Economic Regulation"[25] and Posner's "Taxation by Regulation"[26] but concentrated on detailed empirical and analytical studies of government regulation.[27]

The *Bell Journal* published important articles on Interstate Commerce Commission (ICC) regulation of railroads and trucking,[28] Federal Communications Commission regulation,[29] Federal Power Commission regulation,[30] airline regulation,[31] and the regulation of electricity.[32]

These multiple law and economics articles in the *Journal of Law & Economics* and in the *Bell Journal*, plus other economic treatments,[33] led to a dramatic change of views, approaching a consensus, among academics and among policymakers as to the limited value of extensive government economic regulation. These various articles make two basic points: first, that many of the specific regulations adopted by these agencies did not enhance societal welfare; second, that the policies served to benefit specific firms if not industries. Stigler's, Posner's, and Peltzman's works[34] were important toward this end. Support for many of the regulatory policies criticized in these articles dropped significantly.

In what has become known as the deregulation movement, the ICC, established by Congress in 1887 to regulate railroads and whose jurisdiction was extended in 1935 to include interstate bussing and trucking, all largely criticized in these articles, had its jurisdiction stripped in 1976. The Commission was abolished in 1995 with its sole remaining safety responsibilities shifted to the Department of Transportation. The Federal Power Commission, created in 1930 to regulate interstate electricity and natural gas supply, was eliminated in 1977 and replaced, with sharply limited authority, by the Federal Energy Regulatory Commission. The Civil Aeronautics Board, created in 1938 to regulate airlines,

25 Stigler 1971.

26 Posner 1971b.

27 Again, I only list articles published prior to the mid-1970s.

28 Spann & Erickson 1970; Sloss 1970; Fisher & Kraft 1971; Nelson 1971; Palmer 1973.

29 Littlechild 1970; Chaddha & Chitgopekar 1971; Comanor & Mitchell 1971; Dunn, Williams, & Allen Spivey 1971; Thompson & Tiao 1971; Crandall 1972; Park 1972; Posner 1972a; Artle & Averous 1973; Levin 1973; Squire 1973.

30 MacAvoy 1970; Erickson & Spann 1971; Khazzoom 1971; MacAvoy 1971a; MacAvoy & Pindyck 1973.

31 Keeler 1972; Verleger 1973.

32 Brandon 1971; Litzenberger & Rao 1971; Emery 1973.

33 As an example, Kahn 1970–71.

34 Posner 1971b; Peltzman 1971; Stigler 1971.

had its authority vastly stripped in the Airline Deregulation Act of 1978 and was finally "disestablished" in 1995, with sole remaining safety responsibilities shifted to the Department of Transportation. All of these regulatory changes derived from the sustained economic analysis of these journals. There have been only selective additions to governmental regulation since early 1970,[35] including the 2002 Sarbanes–Oxley corporate governance act, the 2010 Dodd–Frank financial regulation act (though subject to current (2018) reduction), and the 2010 Patient Protection and Affordable Care Act.[36]

The influence on antitrust

As described earlier, papers commissioned by Director—often deriving from Director's ideas[37]—also, criticized then-current antitrust doctrine on similar grounds. During the 1940s, 1950s, and 1960s, the Supreme Court had expanded the range of antitrust offenses, in particular extending the per se prohibition[38] to many practices. The per se prohibition had been first announced in 1940 in a case dealing with price fixing in the oil industry, deriving from the cartel-creating policies of the National Industrial Recovery Act.[39] The Court, adopting the per se approach prohibiting any form of price fixing, later redefined earlier opinions as also establishing per se prohibitions, such as of vertical price fixing (resale price maintenance) (*Dr. Miles* 1911)[40] and group boycotts.[41]

In the subsequent three decades, the Supreme Court vastly expanded antitrust liability by further extending the per se rule to apply to tying agreements,[42] exclusive dealing arrangements,[43] predatory pricing,[44] vertical territorial restrictions,[45] other vertical sales arrangements resembling boycotts,[46] maximum price fixing,[47] and also defined extremely restrictive standards for the approval of vertical mergers.[48]

35 The Occupational Safety and Health Administration was created in 1970, but chiefly to extend labor workplace restrictions. The Consumer Product Safety Commission was created in 1972, but has never been seriously influential. The Transportation Safety Administration was created after 9/11, but is a watchguard not empowered to directly regulate industry.

36 For an excellent review of changes in regulation over the past 40 years, see Van Doren & Firey 2017.

37 For example, McGee 1958; Stigler 1965.

38 The per se prohibition in antitrust law means that no defense can be raised to the claim.

39 *U.S. v. Socony-Vacuum Oil*, 310 U.S. 150 (1940).

40 *Dr. Miles Medical Co. v. John D. Parke & Sons Co.*, 220 U.S. 373 (1911).

41 *Fashion Originator's Guild*, 312 U.S. 457 (1941); *Eastern States Retail Lumber Association*, 234 U.S. 600 (1914).

42 *International Business Machines Corp. v. U.S.*, 298 U.S. 131 (1936); *International Salt Co. v. U.S.*, 332 U.S. 392 (1947); *Northern Pacific Railway Co. v. U.S.*, 356 U.S. 1 (1958).

43 *Standard Oil Co. of California and Standard Stations, Inc v. U.S.*, 337 U.S. 293 (1949).

44 *Utah Pie v. Continental Baking Co.*, 386 U.S. 685 (1967).

45 *U.S. v. Arnold, Schwinn & Co.*, 388 U.S. 365 (1967).

46 *Klor's Inc. v. Broadway-Hale Stores*, 359 U.S. 207 (1959).

47 *Albrecht v. Herald Co.*, 390 U.S. 145 (1968).

48 *Brown Shoe Co. v. U.S.*, 370 U.S. 294 (1962); *U.S. v. Von's Grocery Co.*, 384 U.S. 270 (1966).

Participants in the Antitrust Project at Chicago criticized all of these decisions. Perhaps because Director and his successor as Editor of the *Journal of Law & Economics*, Ronald Coase, were uninterested in the legal process (neither were lawyers), the tone of many of these articles was derisive and generally contemptuous: the Supreme Court and the lower courts, as well as the attorneys for the parties, had not understood the economics; as a result, the ultimate Supreme Court opinions made no sense.

Director had taught a now-legendary class at Chicago with Edward Levi (later the Dean of the Law School, Provost, and President of the University) at which, as the story is told, Levi in four days of lectures would rationalize the Supreme Court's treatment of these issues and Director in the one day allotted him would show that, from an economic standpoint, the Court's (and, indirectly, Levi's) analysis was nonsense.[49] Levi, a moderate, and a highly intelligent man, came around to Director's view of the subject—especially with respect to the great unlikelihood that vertical arrangements could increase market power—and published a seminal article with Director in 1956, "Law and the Future: Trade Regulation," obviously written by Levi.[50]

In the 1970s, law and economics would at least change the attitude of these criticisms. There are many earlier articles published in the *Journal of Law & Economics* criticizing the Supreme Court's analyses of antitrust issues: as described earlier, McGee's criticism of *Standard Oil*; Telser's criticism of *General Electric*; and Dam's, Bowman's, and Peterman's criticisms of the prohibition of tying arrangements, among others.[51]

This continual criticism was summarized and attracted serious legal import through two books published in the 1970s. In 1976 Richard Posner, who had known Director from his year at Stanford, subsequently taught with Director at Chicago, and, of course, was later a colleague of Coase,[52] published *Antitrust Law: An Economic Perspective*, which soberly and fairly addressed the economic weaknesses of the various Supreme Court opinions over these years. Shortly thereafter, in 1978, Robert Bork (Figure 9.1), who had been a Research Associate in Director's Project after law school in the 1950s, published *The Antitrust Paradox: A Policy at War with Itself*, which would cement the view and, I believe, ultimately lead the Supreme Court to overturn its earlier antitrust jurisprudence.

Posner's book presented a chiefly economic analysis of the issues that the Supreme Court had addressed. Bork's book was somewhat different and derived both from Director's ideas about vertical practices and also, importantly, from his work with Alex Bickel at Yale Law School and from his service as Solicitor General.

49 Kitch 1983.

50 Director & Levi 1956.

51 See *supra*, Chapter 4.

52 From personal experience, I do not think that Posner's views on antitrust were importantly influenced by Coase, though Coase as Editor of the *Journal of Law & Economics* published several of Posner's papers, including on antitrust.

FIGURE 9.1 Robert H. Bork, 1979
Photo courtesy of Yale Law School

Bork, appointed by Nixon as Solicitor General, believed strongly that the Supreme Court should apply "neutral principles" in its decisions, meaning that the Court should not be responsive to political issues, but should apply legal principles neutral and defensible.

Bork had earlier written an article in 1968, after leaving Director's Project, published in the *Journal of Law & Economics*, which asserted, on the basis of reading the Congressional discussion, that the original basis of the Sherman Act was to protect consumer welfare.[53] He had drafted a book elaborating these views in 1969, though the book was not published until 1978, because of his wife's illness and his appointment as Solicitor General.

Bork argued, more extensively in 1978 in *The Antitrust Paradox* than in the earlier articles, that the promotion of consumer welfare was a neutral principle that could be implemented by judges without involving judges in essentially political decisions over which interest groups should prevail under industrial organization law. Bork, in this respect, was presenting a theory of judging, obviously related to the academic discussions which had been initiated a decade before over neutral principles following the Supreme Court's decision in 1954 in *Brown v. Board of Education*.[54] With respect to this question, Bork was probably heavily

53 Bork 1968.
54 *Brown v. Board of Education of Topeka*, 347 U.S. 483 (1954). See Wechsler 1959.

influenced by his friendship and work with his Yale Law School colleague Alexander Bickel,[55] with whom Bork taught seminars on constitutional adjudication at Yale for many years.

With this element of Bork's strategy in *The Antitrust Paradox*, Bork differed more substantially from his Chicago School mentor Aaron Director, and from other expositions of the Chicago School analysis of antitrust law, including Richard Posner's *Antitrust Law: An Economic Perspective.*

Bork, in *The Antitrust Paradox*, presented a concept of judging and then applied that concept to jurisprudence under the Sherman Act. First, judges should apply only neutral principles, and not engage in political judgments among competing interest groups, which is the province of Congress. On this point, Bork in *The Antitrust Paradox* is especially critical of Justice Douglas, whose antitrust opinions in the 1960s and 1970s, particularly with regard to vertical restrictions, advocated support of small business and dealer independence, regardless of economic effect. Second, the promotion of consumer welfare is a neutral principle. Third, the promotion of consumer welfare was the original principle adopted by Congress in 1890 with the Sherman Act which Bork claimed to have established in his 1968 article in the *Journal of Law & Economics.*[56] Fourth, the promotion of consumer welfare is the basis for the per se prohibition of price fixing (which all had to endorse). Finally, the Court's then-current prohibitions of various vertical restraints are inconsistent with the promotion of consumer welfare.

In order to appreciate Bork's contribution, it is important to see how his approach extended beyond the Chicago School criticism of antitrust law by his mentor Aaron Director, by the Director–Levi article, by the many articles published in the *Journal of Law & Economics*, and even from Richard Posner's book, which preceded Bork's *Antitrust Paradox* by several years, in presenting the Chicago School criticism. Director and Director–Levi's criticism of then-current antitrust law, as well as many other articles, consisted essentially of economic analyses. The point of these treatments was to demonstrate that there was no defensible economic basis for the many Supreme Court antitrust decisions striking down vertical arrangements.

Posner's approach was slightly different. Posner, in the first edition of *Antitrust Law: An Economic Analysis*, pushed the Supreme Court to adopt more vigorous rules against possible combinations, especially with regard to tacit collusion.

55 See Bickel 1962.

56 Without ever talking to Bork about this, and I know of no writing of his on the subject, I believe Bork's method with respect to interpretation of the Sherman Act is related to his later constitutional scholarship. Bork sought to identify a neutral principle and looked to original intent to define it. Thus, with respect to the Sherman Act, Bork claimed that promoting consumer welfare was the original intent and served as a neutral principle for interpretation of the Act. Bork's extension of this interpretive method to his subsequent constitutional originalism became much more controversial.

Posner and Bork differ little with respect to all other industrial organization issues, especially vertical restraints. But Posner's arguments, as might be expected from a younger scholar, adopted an aggressive style (though Posner remained aggressive as the years went on), pushing the Supreme Court to adopt new rules prohibiting presumed price agreements.

Bork accepted the Chicago School view that there was no coherent economic basis for the various Court prohibitions on vertical agreements. But he went beyond this point. Bork presented a theory of judging: judges should only apply neutral principles. He then explained why the promotion of consumer welfare was a neutral principle, different from the Chicago School argument that the promotion of consumer welfare enhances social welfare generally solely on economic grounds. He then argued, in my view questionably, that the promotion of consumer welfare was the original intent of Congress in enacting the Sherman Act. He deemed that this principle had been subsequently affirmed in *Trans-Missouri* and in the subsequent cases, especially *Addyston Pipe*, and even later in the adoption of the per se prohibition of price fixing.[57] He employed Taft's distinction in *Addyston Pipe* between main and ancillary restraints to argue that all vertical restraints were ancillary to the other purposes of the vertical agreement. Then he argued that adoption of the per se prohibition of price fixing—market creating—was inconsistent with the Court's prohibition of vertical ancillary restraints as well as with the Court's hostility to vertical mergers which were market restricting. This was a novel approach to the understanding of antitrust law.

To my mind, there are two other elements to the success of Bork's efforts. First, as mentioned, the publication of his book *The Antitrust Paradox* was delayed from 1969 to 1978 because of his wife's illness and his necessary response to it (she died of cancer in 1980), and his appointment as Solicitor General in 1973. There is no way to measure or even document this effect, but Bork's service as Solicitor General probably importantly affected the Supreme Court's acceptance of his analysis in *The Antitrust Paradox*. By 1978, in contrast to 1969, the Court knew Bork well. I have not studied this matter, but surely he had appeared before the Court innumerable times.[58] Bork was a person ferociously devoted to principle, had developed a principle for the appropriate manner of judging in a democratic society, was dedicated to advocating what was best for the broader American public rather than for any special interest, and was highly articulate in explaining his views. There is every reason to

57 Stigler among other Chicago School scholars was critical of price fixing and developed a theory of collusion that was highly important, though not relied on heavily by Bork (Stigler 1964).

58 Some years earlier, Richard Posner served in the Solicitor General's Office and had argued antitrust cases before the Court and, before that, had been a clerk to Justice Brennan and is widely viewed as having written the highly influential opinion in *Philadelphia National Bank*. Posner, and his high intelligence, were also known to the Supreme Court. There is no way to compare influence, but Bork's service as Solicitor General involved both a more elevated political position and longer service.

believe that the Supreme Court in 1978 (perhaps in contrast to 1969) understood that the views expressed in *The Antitrust Paradox* derived from a serious and highly principled individual and gave them more respect on those grounds.

Second, in 1974 John Paul Stevens was appointed to the Court, replacing Justice Douglas, who had retired. President Nixon had resigned in 1973. His successor, Gerald Ford, appointed Edward Levi, then President of the University of Chicago, as Attorney General to restore integrity to the office.[59] This was the Levi of Director–Levi. Levi had been a lower school classmate of Stevens and knew him well. Stevens had attended Northwestern Law School, not the University of Chicago, and so had not taken classes from Director, and later became a prominent antitrust attorney in Chicago. Though this has not been previously emphasized, as Levi took on greater administrative duties as Dean of the University of Chicago Law School, later Provost of the University, and even later President, he asked Stevens to take his place in teaching the antitrust class at Chicago with Aaron Director, which Stevens did for apparently two years. Stevens later stated that his teaching the class with Director, like Bork's as a student, was the most important intellectual experience of his life.[60]

On the Supreme Court, Stevens was not a doctrinaire Chicago School advocate. Certainly, he understood and adopted Director's view about vertical restrictions. He authored the Court's opinion in *Fortner II*, rejecting tying arrangement claims. He became, following White, the Supreme Court's designee with respect to antitrust, authoring important opinions largely adopting Chicago School views in *NCAA* (affirming the prohibition of a price fixing and market allocation agreement among non-profit universities), *Jefferson Parish Hospital* (acknowledging efficiencies from tying arrangements), and *Aspen Skiing* (finding a monopolization violation deriving entirely from Bork's *Antitrust Paradox*, but, in my view, misreading Bork.)[61]

But, again, Justice Stevens was not devoted entirely to the Chicago School approach. Among other deviations, he joined the dissent in *Leegin*, voting to retain the per se prohibition of resale price maintenance, though largely on grounds of preserving precedent: the prohibition had been first announced in 1911 and had survived various Congressional efforts to overturn it.

Nevertheless, it is likely that Stevens influenced the Supreme Court's adoption of Bork's views in *The Antitrust Paradox*. At the minimum, Stevens' seriousness and intellectual power were likely to have convinced the other members of the Court that the Chicago School criticism of antitrust law was not the lunatic fringe, which many other academics had argued.[62] It has not

59 Two of Nixon's Attorneys General—John Mitchell and Richard Kleindienst—had been indicted for criminal offenses, and the former was ultimately jailed for his role in Watergate.

60 See Priest & Levi 2010. Edward Levi's grandson, William Levi, a student in my Antitrust class, alerted me to this fact, for which I am very grateful.

61 See Priest & Lewinsohn 2007 at 229.

62 See, for example, Lande 1989.

been currently documented how well Bork and Stevens knew each other or the extent to which Stevens had accepted Bork's views. But surely the appointment of a (not then known) largely Chicago School antitrust lawyer to the Supreme Court must have affected its analysis of antitrust issues.

The Supreme Court's change of antitrust law doctrine and its progressive adoption of the Chicago School approach can be dated from the Court's 1977 opinion in *Pueblo Bowl-O-Mat*,[63] greatly restricting private antitrust actions by firms harmed by competition. There is little evidence, however, of direct Chicago School influence on that opinion. More indelible forms of evidence of Chicago School influence on the Court's change in doctrine are the Court's opinions in the same year in *Fortner II*,[64] as mentioned, in an opinion written by John Paul Stevens overturning the Court's previous acceptance of a tying arrangement claim,[65] and in *GTE-Sylvania*,[66] acknowledging the benefits of vertical territorial restrictions, overruling the per se prohibition of those restrictions in *Schwinn* (1967). In *GTE-Sylvania*, Posner and Bork were cited repeatedly.[67]

In succeeding years, the Supreme Court progressively extended the Chicago School analysis. For example, in 1979, in *Reiter v. Sonotone*, the Court explicitly adopted the Chicago School (Bork) approach of defining the ambition of antitrust law as promoting consumer welfare.[68] In 1984, in *Jefferson Parish Hospital*, the Court restricted the per se prohibition of tying arrangements, with four Justices (a minority) voting to eliminate the per se prohibition entirely.[69] In 1986, in *Matsushita*, and in 1993, in *Brooke Group*,[70] the Court vastly increased the evidentiary findings necessary to prove predatory pricing. In 1997, in *State Oil v. Kahn*, the Court overturned the per se prohibition of maximum price fixing.[71] The Court continued to announce standards restricting claims of minimum price fixing, established in the 1911 *Dr. Miles* case,[72] finally overturning the per se prohibition of the practice in 2007 in *Leegin*, extensively citing Bork and Posner.[73] In all of these opinions, as mentioned, the Court cited Posner and Bork, often effusively, not just as footnotes but as part of the Court's textual analysis; for example, "As then-Professor Bork explained ..."[74] and "As Judge Bork has noted ..."[75]

63 *Brunswick Corp. v. Pueblo Bowl-O-Mat, Inc.*, 429 U.S. 477 (1977).

64 *Fortner II, supra* n. 60.

65 See Dam 1969.

66 *Continental T.V., Inc. v. GTE Sylvania, Inc.*, 433 U.S. 36 (1977).

67 *GTE Sylvania, Inc.*, at 56, 66, 69 (1977).

68 *Reiter v. Sonotone Corp*, 442 U.S. 330 (1979).

69 *Jefferson Parish Hospital District No. 2 v. Hyde*, 466 U.S. 2 (1984).

70 Bork argued the *Brooke Group* case on behalf of the prevailing defendant.

71 *State Oil v. Kahn*, 522 U.S. 3 (1997).

72 *Dr. Miles Medical Co. v. John D. Park & Sons Co.*, 220 U.S. 373 (1911). See *Business Electronics Corp. v. Sharp Electronics Corp.*, 485 U.S. 717(1988); *Monsanto v. Spray-Rite*, 465 U.S. 752 (1984).

73 *Leegin Creative Leather Products, Inc. v. PSKS, Inc.*, 551 U.S. 877, 881, 890, 898, 915 (2007).

74 *Matsushita, supra* n. For a further elaboration of this argument, see Priest 2014b.

75 *National Collegiate Athletic Ass'n. v. Board of Regents of University of Oklahoma*, 469 U.S. 85 (1984).

The changes in the conception of regulation and in antitrust doctrine over these years have been profound. The changes in regulation—the deregulation movement—reflect a new understanding of how regulation might help or hurt consumers. The changes in antitrust doctrine represent, essentially, a complete rejection of the antitrust law that the Supreme Court had established in scores of opinions from the 1940s to the mid-1970s. Posner and Bork, as mentioned, were cited and relied upon continuously during this change. Their views derived from, but added to, the ideas of Aaron Director. The influence of these ideas and of law and economics scholarship concerning these fields has totally overturned these fields.

10

HENRY MANNE AND THE POPULAR EXPANSION OF LAW AND ECONOMICS

Henry Manne was an important academic in law and economics but, more importantly, an extraordinary entrepreneur with respect to the field. After an early career in academics that was highly productive, he shifted to academic administration, chiefly with the idea of promoting law and economics. He founded several law and economics programs and, later, became Dean of a law school where he directed the curriculum to law and economics subjects. His most significant achievement in my mind, however, was obtaining support for the organizing of programs to teach economics to law professors, to teach law to economics professors and, most importantly in terms of the significance of his work, to teach law and economics to federal judges. Manne also organized theme programs for legal academics and economists discussing topics central then to law and economics, which enhanced the network of the field.

These various programs built on the academic successes of Coase, Calabresi, and Posner, though also of others. Manne never emphasized the work of Calabresi and Posner, though he did of Coase and, in particular, the implications of Coase's analysis with respect to the definition of property rights. Manne's programs vastly expanded the reach of law and economics.

Manne received his law degree from the University of Chicago and later received a JSD from Yale which he never emphasized. He recounts that he was importantly influenced by Aaron Director and of the pervasiveness of economic thought at Chicago.[1] He subsequently taught at American University in Washington and published several important—indeed, seminal—articles on corporate organization. His work was economic from the outset. He developed two

1 Kitch 1983 at 184.

extremely important ideas: the market for corporate control and the benefits of insider trading.

Manne wrote several articles identifying the market for corporate control: that there exists a market in corporate acquisitions that will serve to discipline corporate officers to manage their corporations to achieve the highest benefit. This idea rejected the dominant theory of the time of Berle and Means that corporate directors, insulated from shareholders, had different (often personal) maximizing objectives.[2]

Manne made this point repeatedly in many articles, both in legal journals[3] and in the prominent *Journal of Political Economy*.[4] The idea was of sufficient significance that some scholars have dated use of the term "the market for corporate control" from Manne's original article.[5]

Manne also had innovative ideas about insider trading: the purchase or sale of stock by corporate officers who, presumably, possessed greater information about the prospects of the stock they were trading than did outside investors. The practice had been widely condemned as unfair to outside investors who did not possess equivalent information. Manne made the point, first, that insider trading served to compensate insiders and to align their interests with the fortunes of the corporation. He made a second point that insider trading by corporate managers, when revealed, provided important information to outside investors as to the prospects of the corporation.[6] Manne's views on this point have been largely, though not entirely, adopted by academics, but not (yet) by the courts.

These academic contributions are not at all insignificant in the field of corporate law, but Manne's more extensive contributions derive from his nearly lifelong efforts to promote and expand the field of law and economics.

The economist Allen Wallis had been the Dean of the University of Chicago Business School and a colleague and close friend of Stigler, Director, and others. In 1962, he was appointed President of the University of Rochester. In 1968, Rochester hired Henry Manne as the William R. Kenan, Jr. Professor of Law and Political Science, where his principal role was to create a law school of which he would become the dean. Manne saw the law school—and Wallis surely concurred with this—as specializing in law and economics. Before creating the law school, Manne began his Economic Institutes for Law Professors at which, over a period of two weeks, prominent economists such as Armen Alchian and Harold Demsetz taught basic economic principles to law professors interested in learning something about law and economics.[7] Later, he would

2 Berle & Means 1932.

3 Manne 1962, 1967a, 1967b.

4 Manne 1965.

5 Carney 1999.

6 Manne 1966a, 1966b.

7 See, for example, Schwartz (who attended the first of these Institutes) 1999. See also Teles 2008 at 102–103.

create similar "Law for Economists" Institute at which law professors would teach economists about the law.[8]

However successful Manne's Economic and Law Institutes,[9] the Rochester law school project ran into trouble, apparently because of funding difficulties and resistance from the local bar association.[10] The law school was never founded at Rochester.

In 1974, Manne moved to the University of Miami, where he founded a Law and Economics Center, affiliated with the Law School, the Economics Department, and the Graduate School of Business. Within the Center, Manne continued his programs of Economics and Law Institutes and expanded separate programs with the support of the Liberty Fund (described further below). He recruited many prominent economists to the Center: Ken Clarkson, Don Martin, and Louis DiAlessi, among others, and received funding from the John M. Olin Foundation for scholarships to fund the law school tuitions of Ph. D economics candidates. The importance of the John M. Olin Foundation to the rise of law and economics is discussed in Chapter 11.

Manne's Economics Institutes for Law Professors and his comparable programs teaching law to economists had extraordinary success. By 1999, over 1,000 professors had attended these programs.[11] Though these Institutes were important to the academic extension of law and economics, Manne sought broader influence. Perhaps most important was his establishment of Economics Institutes for Federal Judges. These, too, consisted of roughly two-week sessions at which prominent economists and lawyer-economists would teach basic economics principles to judges (Figure 10.1). Manne recruited outstanding economists, including those of different political persuasions, to teach in these programs, including the Nobel laureates Milton Friedman, Paul Samuelson, and Kenneth Arrow. By 1990, 40 percent of then-sitting federal judges had attended Manne's programs.[12] One Court of Appeals Judge wrote, "Dean Henry G. Manne has made a greater contribution to the continuing professional education of America's federal judges than any individual, foundation, institute or agency in the nation."[13]

Over the same twenty-year period, Manne also organized shorter conferences for legal and economics scholars sponsored by the Liberty Fund. These conferences—from 1975 to 1997, there were forty-four of them—were devoted to a single topic with papers presented by leading scholars followed by commentary by the assembled group.[14]

8 These programs continue today sponsored by George Mason University Law School.
9 See Rubin 1999.
10 Teles 2008 at 105.
11 Butler 1999.
12 Butler 1999 at 352.
13 Judge James L. Ryan, 6th Circuit Court of Appeals Judge, quoted in Butler 1999 at 351.
14 Rubin 1999.

FIGURE 10.1 Henry Manne and the judges. First row, third from right, Henry Manne; fourth from right, Henry Friendly; third from left, Martin Feldstein. Second row, third from left, Paul Samuelson; fourth from left, Armen Alchian.
Photo courtesy of George Mason University Antonin Scalia Law School

Manne had a style for these conferences (as well as for his various Institutes): they were held at exotic U.S. locations (after he moved to Miami, chiefly on Florida islands) with a small, selected, number of invitees; honoraria for those presenting papers or teaching; and good food.

These amenities attracted the academics and the judges.

For the academics, the conferences were attractive enough in themselves. Prior to Manne's innovation of them, conferences were very rare in academics, especially in legal academics. Putting aside Manne and his successors, they remain rare today. It is very common for social scientists to list conferences attended as a separate category on their resumes, with two or three entries for even an experienced scholar. Many of my colleagues at the various law schools at which I have taught had never been invited to a topical conference, attending only the annual meeting of the trade association (Association of American Law Schools).

The importance of Manne's academic contributions has been described. The importance to the rise of law and economics of Manne's "administrative"—better, entrepreneurial—contributions—especially his Economics and Law Institutes, Economic Institutes for Federal Judges, and the multiple Liberty Fund Conferences—has been, perhaps, greater.

This book has emphasized the originality of ideas to the rise of law and economics: Director's criticisms of regulation and antitrust law, Coase's brilliant conception of the role of the market in affecting the implications of legal decisions, Calabresi's innovative formulation of an economic model for evaluating legal rules, Posner's demonstration that economic analysis enhanced the understanding of all of the law. These and many other contributions were highly original and were efforts of high intellectual achievement.

But the contributions to the spread of these original ideas should not be underestimated. Director spread his ideas, not personally, but through his Antitrust program, recruiting highly talented scholars such as Bork, MacAvoy, Bowman, McGee, and others, and through his influence on Edward Levi and John Paul Stevens; and, of course, through his editorship of the *Journal of Law & Economics*.

Coase continued Director's Antitrust program (in which I was a Research Associate, vastly enhancing my career), but turned his academic interests to

FIGURE 10.2 Seminar on the Intellectual History of Law and Economics. Los Angeles, March 5–8, 1981. First row, left to right: Rose D. Friedman, Milton Friedman. Second row: Bernard H. Siegan (San Diego), Harold Demsetz, Michael J. Trebilcock, Aaron Director, Ronald H. Coase, Henry G. Manne, Gary S. Becker. Third row: Walter Blum, Richard O. Zerbe (U. Washington), Kenneth E. Scott (Stanford), Sam Peltzman, Steven N.S. Cheung. Fourth row: John S. McGee, Williams H. Adams, III, Jesse Markham. Fifth row, Ward Bowman, Armen Alchian, Edmund W. Kitch, Richard A. Posner, Robert H. Bork. Sixth row: Wesley J. Liebeler, George L. Priest, W. Allen Wallis, George J. Stigler, Benjamin Klein, William M. Landes, Thomas D. Morgan

other subjects. Harold Demsetz and others contributed to the understanding of the significance of Coase's ideas.

Calabresi only modestly spread his ideas, turning to other, possibly more profound ethical issues. Posner spread his ideas widely through massive publications and the continued editions of *Economic Analysis of Law*.

It takes time for academic ideas to influence the world. Director's ideas of the late-1940s and 1950s were subsequently implemented after Bork's book in the late-1970s. As a student, after a class with Ronald Coase in which he explained his idea of the federal government auctioning off TV and radio frequencies, I asked him: this seems so obvious, why hasn't it been adopted? Ronald replied: give it 30 years. It took 40 years for the government to come around to auctioning off frequencies, but his was a good approximation.

Henry Manne's various conferences and Institutes for economics professors, law professors, and judges significantly accelerated this process and advanced the field (Figure 10.2).

11

EPILOGUE

The John M. Olin Foundation and the founding of the American Law and Economics Association

The John M. Olin Foundation, especially under the direction of its President, James R. Piereson, was an extraordinary sponsor of law and economics and greatly contributed to its success. The Foundation had given early grants to Henry Manne for his economics programs for law professors and had provided grants for professorships, at various universities, for prominent scholars, such as Walter Berns at Georgetown and James Q. Wilson at UCLA.[1]

In the mid-1980s, however, the Foundation broadened its support for the field, by giving grants for the study of law and economics to several major law schools. Chicago was given a grant in 1985. Yale Law School received a three-year grant for a law and economics program in 1985;[2] Harvard, Stanford, and others, shortly thereafter. These various law and economics programs typically provided support for faculty fellowships—outside faculty given a year's leave for work at the host law school—student fellowships, and occasional conferences.[3]

In the succeeding years, as the field of law and economics was expanding built on the achievements of Coase, Calabresi, Posner, and others from the 1960s through the 1980s, there was substantial talk among members of the field about the formation

1 These professorships were not endowed. The Olin Foundation did not believe in endowments—to my knowledge, none of its gifts to law and economics programs were endowed—because endowments ceded later control over the use of such funds, often citing the Ford Foundation endowments from whose board Henry Ford II resigned in 1976 on the grounds that the Foundation was pursuing interests different from those of its founder. I was offered an Olin Professorship at UCLA in 1984, but turned it down.

2 Yale Law School received an additional three-year grant to name me the John M. Olin Professor in 1986. It was subsequently renewed through 2009. The Olin Foundation closed, as had been specified by its donor to avoid problems such as those of the Ford Foundation, in 2005.

3 See Teles 2008 at 188–191 and Figure 6.1 at 201.

of a more formal law and economics association. The founding of such an association would require substantial administrative effort and most law and economics scholars, intent on pursuing their academic work, declined to pursue the task. Much of the talk centered on the directors of two law and economics programs as possible candidates to organize a general association: Henry Manne, the extraordinary entrepreneur of law and economics programs, then Dean at George Mason Law School; and Priest, at Yale Law School. But efforts lagged for many years.

In 1990, Henry Manne took the lead and secured a grant from the John M. Olin Foundation to support the organization of such an association. With the grant, Manne convened an organizing session with directors of other Olin law and economics programs, such as Priest of Yale, Polinsky of Stanford, and Shavell of Harvard, with other law and economics scholars, including Cooter of Berkeley and Ulen of Illinois (authors of a leading law and economics textbook), Trebilcock of the University of Toronto, and others, to discuss the organization of such an association, held at George Mason Law School.

At the organizing meeting, there was unanimous support for the founding of such an association. A strong difference of opinion among the group emerged, however, as to its structure and, in particular, what would be the nature of the annual meeting that the association would hold, its only important event. Henry Manne vigorously pressed for an association and an annual meeting modeled on the style of the Liberty Fund conferences he had run for many years, described in Chapter 10: a limited number of selected academic invitees—twenty or so—held in attractive resort locations, with selected judges and attorneys also invited to attend.

A separate faction, headed by Priest, along with Shavell and Polinsky, wanted the new law and economics association to be modeled on the American Economic Association, with open attendance by academics, the presentation of submitted papers in convened panels, discussion open to all attending, with no particular representation of judges or attorneys.

Through meetings lasting the entire day discussing a range of administrative matters, the issue of organization of the association's annual meeting was not finally resolved. The agenda for the organizing meeting, however, provided that, at the end of the day, the assembled group was to select the first President of what was to become the American Law and Economics Association. Late in the afternoon, Manne encouraged the group to get going with the election, since cocktails were about to be served at a party at his house. (He was a generous host.) Reflecting the earlier debate, the two candidates for President were Henry Manne and Priest.

After substantial deliberation,[4] the group chose Manne to be the President of the new Association, but with an Administrative Council—supposedly to advise him—consisting of Priest, Shavell, and Polinsky.

4 The two candidates were excused. Henry Manne and I were out in the hall as the remaining group debated over the presidency, and I said to him, "This Association should be larger, and not simply part of the Henry Manne empire." He responded, aggressively, with his arms pushed up, "Why not?" This encouraged my resolve with respect to the Association.

Manne hosted a gracious cocktail party at his home and an outside dinner. After returning to the hotel, however, Polinsky, Shavell, and Priest met in Polinsky's hotel room. None was satisfied with the group's resolution of the dispute over what the Association was to be or over its leadership. After extended discussion, the three agreed to address Jim Piereson of the Olin Foundation with the issue.

When Priest returned home the next morning, a Sunday, he drafted a letter to Jim Piereson, explaining the debate and the view of Shavell, Polinsky, and Priest as to the appropriate outcome, and faxed it to Shavell and Polinsky. The three talked by conference call and agreed that, instead of the letter,[5] Priest should call Jim Piereson and explain the situation.

Priest called Piereson the next day. It was important to Piereson that Polinsky and Shavell agreed with Priest's objections to the Henry Manne plan. Shortly thereafter, Piereson, on behalf of the John M. Olin Foundation, revoked the remaining grant to Manne and transferred it to Priest.

In the months after, Priest went through the bureaucratic work: hiring a lawyer, getting the Association incorporated, drafting bylaws, etc. Priest also organized the program of what would be the first Meeting of the American Law and Economics Association.

It was planned that, at this first Association Meeting, the attendees—then members of the new Association—would choose officers of the Association—according to the bylaws, President, Vice-President, Treasurer—and members of a Board of Directors.

Quite fortunately, Tom Ulen offered to host the first Association Meeting at the University of Illinois, Champaign-Urbana. Priest, anticipating being a candidate for President, did not want the Meeting at Yale.

At the first Meeting of the American Law and Economics Association, 200 academics attended. Priest organized a Plenary Session for the Meeting to honor four founders of law and economics as a discipline: Ronald Coase, Guido Calabresi, Richard Posner, and Henry Manne. All attended. Guido Calabresi, returning from Italy, was late, but when he arrived, he galloped down the main aisle, waiting to be introduced.

With respect to the election of the first President of the Association and its succession, Priest had put together a slate of candidates, including Bill Landes as Vice-President (to succeed Priest after one year), Mitch Polinsky as Treasurer, and many other distinguished law and economics scholars to serve on the Board of Directors, some of whom (Shavell, Cooter, and Trebilcock, among others) had attended Henry Manne's organizing session.

It was expected that Henry Manne would run in opposition, and there was a late registry of George Mason scholars to the Meeting, which expanded the intrigue. But Manne did not run.

As mentioned, there are now 656 members of the American Law and Economics Association. In 2019, 483 papers were submitted for presentation at the Association's 28th Annual Meeting.

5 The draft of the letter is lost in some earlier floppy disk.

TABLE OF CASES

BIBLIOGRAPHY

AALS and Emory University Law and Economics Center. October 28–30, 1982 (Denver, CO). "Symposium Proceedings Published in 1983." *Journal of Legal Education* 33, no. 2 (June 1983): 437–441.

Aivazian, Varouj A., and Jeffrey L. Callen. 1981. "The Coase Theorem and the Empty Core." *Journal of Law and Economics* 24, no. 1 (April): 175–181.

Arnold, Thurman W. 1937. *The Folklore of Capitalism*. New Haven, CT: Yale University Press.

Arnold, Thurman W. 1940. *The Bottlenecks of Business*. New York: Reynal & Hitchcock.

Artle, Roland, and Christian Averous. 1973. "The Telephone System as a Public Good: Static and Dynamic Aspects." *Bell Journal of Economics* 4, no. 1 (Spring): 89–100.

Bagley, Edgar S. 1961. "Water Rights Law and Public Policies Relating to Ground Water Mining in the Southwestern States." *Journal of Law & Economics* 4: 144–174.

Bajt, Aleksander. 1968. "Property in Capital and in the Means of Production in Socialist Economies." *Journal of Law & Economics* 11, no. 1: 1–4.

Baxter, William F., and Lillian R. Altree. 1972. "Legal Aspects of Airport Noise." *Journal of Law & Economics* 15, no. 1: 1–113.

Becker, Gary S. 1968. "Crime and Punishment: An Economic Approach." *Journal of Political Economy* 76, no. 2: 169–217.

Becker, Gary S. 1971. *The Economics of Discrimination*. 2nd ed. Chicago, IL and London: Chicago University Press.

Becker, Gary S. 1976. *The Economic Approach to Human Behavior*. Chicago, IL and London: University of Chicago Press.

Becker, Gary S. 1981. *A Treatise on the Family*. Cambridge, MA: Harvard University Press.

Benham, Lee. 1972. "The Effect of Advertising on the Price of Eyeglasses." *Journal of Law & Economics* 15, no. 2: 337–352.

Berle, Adolf A., Jr., and Gardiner C. Means. 1932. *The Modern Corporation and Private Property*. New York: Macmillan.

Besen, Stanley M. 1974. "The Economics of the Cable Television 'Consensus'." *Journal of Law & Economics* 17, no. 1: 39–51.

Bickel, Alexander. 1962. *The Least Dangerous Branch: The Supreme Court at the Bar of Politics*. Indianapolis and New York: Bobbs-Merrill.

Blum, Walter J., and Harry Kalven. 1964. "Public Law Perspectives on a Private Law Problem: Auto Compensation Plans." *University of Chicago Law Review* 31, no. 4: 641–723.

Bohlen, Francis H. 1905a. "The Basis of Affirmative Obligations in the Law of Tort." *American Law Register (1898–1907)* 53, no. 4 (April): 209–239.

Bohlen, Francis H. 1905b. "The Basis of Affirmative Obligations in the Law of Tort." *American Law Register (1898–1907)* 53, no. 5 (May): 273–310.

Bohlen, Francis H. 1905c. "The Basis of Affirmative Obligations in the Law of Tort." *American Law Register (1898–1907)* 53, no. 6 (June): 337–377.

Bohlen, Francis H. 1912. "A Problem in the Drafting of Workmen's Compensation Acts." *Harvard Law Review* 25, no. 6: 517–547.

Bohlen, Francis H. 1937. "Fifty Years of Torts." *Harvard Law Review* 50, no. 8: 1225–1248.

Bork, Robert H. 1954. "Vertical Integration and the Sherman Act: The Legal History of an Economic Misconception." *University of Chicago Law Review* 22, no. 1: 157–201.

Bork, Robert H. 1968. "Legislative Intent and the Policy of the Sherman Act." *Journal of Law & Economics* 9: 7–48.

Bork, Robert H. 1978. *The Antitrust Paradox*. New York: Basic Books.

Bowman, Ward. 1966. "The New Haven: A Passenger Railroad for Nonriders." *Journal of Law & Economics* 9: 49–59.

Bowman, Ward S. 1955. "The Prerequisites and Effects of Resale Price Maintenance." *University of Chicago Law Review* 22, no. 4: 825–873.

Bowman, Ward S. 1957. "Tying Arrangements and the Leverage Problem." *Yale Law Journal* 67, no. 1: 19–36.

Bowman, Ward S. 1967. "Restraint of Trade by the Supreme Court: The Utah Pie Case." *Yale Law Journal* 77, no. 1: 70–85.

Bowman, Ward S. 1973. *Patent and Antitrust Law: A Legal and Economic Appraisal*. Chicago, IL: University of Chicago Press.

Brandon, Paul S. 1971. "The Electric Side of Combination Gas-Electric Utilities." *Bell Journal of Economics and Management Science* 2, no. 2: 688–703.

Brozen, Yale. 1962. "Minimum Wage Rates and Household Workers." *Journal of Law & Economics* 5: 103–110.

Buchanan, James M. 1959. "Positive Economics, Welfare Economics, and Political Economy." *Journal of Law & Economics* 2 (October): 124–138.

Buchanan, James M. 1974. "Good Economics. Bad Law." *Virginia Law Review* 60, no. 3: 483–492.

Butler, Henry N. 1999. "The Manne Programs in Economics for Federal Judges." *Case Western Reserve Law Review* 50, no. 2: 351–420.

Calabresi, Guido. 1961. "Some Thoughts on Risk Distribution and the Law of Torts." *Yale Law Journal* 70, no. 4: 499–553.

Calabresi, Guido. 1968. "Transaction Costs, Resource Allocation and Liability Rules: A Comment." *Journal of Law & Economics* 11, no. 1: 67–73.

Calabresi, Guido. 1970. *The Costs of Accidents: A Legal and Economic Analysis*. New Haven, CT: Yale University Press.

Calabresi, Guido. 1971. "The New York Plan: A Free Choice Modification." *Columbia Law Review* 71, no. 2 (February): 267–273.

Calabresi, Guido. 1974a. "Birth, Death, and the Law." *Pharos of Alpha Omega Alpha-Honor Medical Society* 37 (April): 39–41.

Calabresi, Guido. 1974b. "Comment on Arrow, Kenneth, 'Government Decision Making & the Preciousness of Life.'" In *Ethics of Health Care*, ed. L.R. Tancredi National Academy of Sciences. Papers of the Conference on Health Care and Changing Values, 48–55. Washington, DC: Institute of Medicine.

Calabresi, Guido. 1975a. "Altruism and Economic Theory, A Comment." In *Altruism, Morality and Economic Theory*, ed. Edmund Phelps, 57–62. New York: Russell Sage Foundation.

Calabresi, Guido. 1975b. "Concerning Cause and the Law of Torts: An Essay for Harry Kalven, Jr." *University of Chicago Law Review* 43, no. 1: 69–108.

Calabresi, Guido. 1975c. "Optimal Deterrence and Accidents: To Fleming James, Jr., Il Miglior Fabbro." *Yale Law Journal* 84, no. 4: 656–671.

Calabresi, Guido. 1978. "Incentives, Regulation, and the Problem of Legal Obsolescence." In *New Perspectives for a Common Law of Europe*, ed. M. Cappelletti, 291–307. Publications of the European University Institute. Leyden/London: Sijthoff.

Calabresi, Guido. 1979. "Access to Justice and Substantive Law Reform: Legal Aid for the Middle Class." In *Access to Justice, Volume III: Emerging Issues and Perspectives*, eds. Mauro Cappelletti and Bryant Garth, 169–190. Leyden/Boston: Sijthoff and Milan: Giuffre.

Calabresi, Guido. 1981. "You Can Call It Thucydides or You Can Call It Mustard Plaster, But It's All Proximate Cause Just the Same!" *Yale Law Journal* 91, no. 1: 1–4.

Calabresi, Guido. 1982. *A Common Law for the Age of Statutes*. Cambridge, MA: Harvard University Press.

Calabresi, Guido. 1985. "Too Much, Too Little, or Both: Some Thoughts on Law Making by American Courts." In *The Cambridge Lectures 1983*, ed. Elizabeth G. Baldwin, 1–17. Toronto: Butterworths.

Calabresi, Guido. 2016. *The Future of Law and Economics: Essays in Reform and Recollection*. New Haven, CT and London: Yale University Press.

Calabresi, Guido, and Philip Bobbitt. 1978. *Tragic Choices*. New York: W.W. Norton & Company.

Calabresi, Guido, and A. Douglas Melamed. 1972. "Property Rules, Liability Rules, and Inalienability: One View of the Cathedral." *Harvard Law Review* 85, no. 6: 1089–1128.

Calabresi, Guido, and Jon T. Hirschoff. 1972. "Toward a Test for Strict Liability in Torts." *Yale Law Journal* 81, no. 6 (May): 1055–1085.

Carney, William J. 1999. "The Legacy of 'The Market for Corporate Control' and the Origins of the Theory of the Firm." *Case Western Reserve Law Review* 50, no. 2: 215–244.

Chaddha, Roshan L., and Sharad S. Chitgopekar. 1971. "A 'Generalization' of the Logistic Curves and Long-Range Forecasts (1966–1991) of Residence Telephones." *Bell Journal of Economics and Management Science* 2, no. 2: 542–560.

Coase, R.H. 1937. "The Nature of the Firm." *Economica, New Series* 4, no. 16: 386–405.

Coase, R.H. 1946. "The Marginal Cost Controversy." *Economica, New Series* 13, no. 51: 69–82.

Coase, R.H. 1950. *British Broadcasting: A Study in Monopoly*. London: Longmans, Green and the London School of Economics.

Coase, R.H. 1959. "The Federal Communications Commission." *Journal of Law & Economics* 2: 1–40.

Coase, R.H. 1960. "The Problem of Social Cost." *Journal of Law & Economics* 3 (October): 1–44.

Coase, R.H. 1961. "The British Post Office and the Messenger Companies." *Journal of Law & Economics* 4: 12–65.

Coase, R.H. 1972. "Durability and Monopoly." *Journal of Law & Economics* 15, no. 1: 143–149.

Coase, R.H. 1974. "The Lighthouse in Economics." *Journal of Law & Economics* 17, no. 2: 357–376.

Coase, R.H. 1988. *The Firm, the Market, and the Law*. Chicago, IL: University of Chicago Press.

Coase, R.H. 1991; 2014. "'The Institutional Structure of Production' (Nobel Prize Address in 1991)." In *Ronald H. Coase*. Coase Sandor Institute of Law and Economics, 137–145. Chicago, IL: University of Chicago Law School.

Coase, R.H. 1993a. "Law and Economics at Chicago." *The Journal of Law & Economics* 36, no. 1: 239–254.

Coase, R.H. 1993b. "Coase on Posner on Coase: Comment." *Journal of Institutional and Theoretical Economics (Jite)/Zeitschrift für die gesamte Staatswissenschaft* 149, no. 1: 96–98.

Coase, R.H. 1998. "The New Institutional Economics." *American Economic Review* 88, no. 2: 72–74.

Coase, R.H. 2000. "The Acquisition of Fisher Body by General Motors." *Journal of Law & Economics* 43, no. 1: 15–32.

Cohen, Morris R. 1916. "Review of *an Introduction to the Philosophy of Law*, by Roscoe Pound." *Columbia Law Review* 22: 774–778.

Colberg, Marshall R. 1960. "Minimum Wage Effects on Florida's Economic Development." *Journal of Law & Economics* 3: 106–117.

Comanor, William S., and Bridger M. Mitchell. 1971. "Cable Television and the Impact of Regulation." *Bell Journal of Economics and Management Science* 2, no. 1: 154–212.

Comanor, William S., and Bridger M. Mitchell. 1972. "The Costs of Planning: The FCC and Cable Television." *Journal of Law & Economics* 15, no. 1: 177–206.

Committee to Study Compensation for Automobile Accidents. 1932. *Report to the Columbia University Council for Research in the Social Sciences*. Philadelphia, PA: Press of International Printing Co.

Cooley, Thomas M., II. 1941. "Problems in Contributory Negligence." *University of Pennsylvania Law Review and American Law Register* 89, no. 3: 335–359.

Crandall, Robert W. 1971. "The Economic Effect of Television-Network Program 'Ownership'." *Journal of Law & Economics* 14, no. 2: 385–412.

Crandall, Robert W. 1972. "FCC Regulation, Monopsony, and Network Television Program Costs." *Bell Journal of Economics and Management Science* 3, no. 2: 483–508.

Crecine, John P., Otto A. Davis, and John E. Jackson. 1967. "Urban Property Markets: Some Empirical Results and Their Implications for Municipal Zoning." *Journal of Law & Economics* 10: 79–99.

Crutchfield, James A. 1961. "An Economic Evaluation of Alternative Methods of Fishery Regulation." *Journal of Law & Economics* 4: 131–143.

Dam, Kenneth W. 1963. "The Economics and Law of Price Discrimination: Herein of Three Regulatory Schemes." *University of Chicago Law Review* 31, no. 1: 1–62.

Dam, Kenneth W. 1965. "Oil and Gas Licensing and the North Sea." *Journal of Law & Economics* 8 (October): 51–75.

Dam, Kenneth W. 1969. "Fortner Enterprises V. United States Steel: 'Neither a Borrower, Nor a Lender Be'." *Supreme Court Review* 1969: 1–40.

Dam, Kenneth W. 1970. "The Pricing of North Sea Gas in Britain." *Journal of Law & Economics* 13, no. 1: 11–44.

Dam, Kenneth W. 1971. "Implementation of Import Quotas: The Case of Oil." *Journal of Law & Economics* 14, no. 1: 1–60.

Dam, Kenneth W. 1974. "The Evolution of North Sea Licensing Policy in Britain and Norway." *Journal of Law & Economics* 17, no. 2: 213–263.

Davies, David G. 1971. "The Efficiency of Public versus Private Firms, the Case of Australia's Two Airlines." *Journal of Law & Economics* 14, no. 1: 149–165.

Demsetz, Harold. 1968. "Why Regulate Utilities?" *Journal of Law & Economics* 11, no. 1: 55–65.

Demsetz, Harold. 1972a. "When Does the Rule of Liability Matter?" *Journal of Legal Studies* 1, no. 1: 13–28.

Demsetz, Harold. 1972b. "Wealth Distribution and the Ownership of Rights." *Journal of Legal Studies* 1, no. 2 (June): 223–232.

Diamond, Peter A. 1974. "Posner's Economic Analysis of Law." *Bell Journal of Economics and Management Science* 5, no. 1: 294–300.

Director, Aaron., and Edward Hirsch Levi. 1956. "Law and the Future: Trade Regulation." *Northwestern University Law Review* 51: 281–296.

Domnarski, William. 2016. *Richard Posner*. New York: Oxford University Press.

Douglas, William O. 1929a. "Vicarious Liability and Administration of Risk I." *Yale L. J.* 38, no. 5: 584–604.

Douglas, William O. 1929b. "Vicarious Liability and Administration of Risk II." *Yale L. J.* 38, no. 6: 720–745.

Dunn, Douglas M., William H. Williams, and W. Allen Spivey. 1971. "Analysis and Prediction of Telephone Demand in Local Geographical Areas." *Bell Journal of Economics and Management Science* 2, no. 2: 561–576.

Dworkin, Ronald M. 1980. "Is Wealth a Value?" *Journal of Legal Studies* 9, no. 2 (March): 191–226.

Eldredge, Laurence H. 1941. "Vendors' Tort Liability." *University of Pennsylvania Law Review* 89, no. 3 (January): 306–334.

Eldredge, Laurence H. 1943. "Francis Hermann Bohlen." *University of Pennsylvania Law Review and American Law Register* 91, no. 5: 387–393.

Emery, E. David. 1973. "Regulated Utilities and Equipment Manufacturers' Conspiracies in the Electrical Power Industry." *Bell Journal of Economics and Management Science* 4, no. 1: 322–337.

Erickson, Edward W., and Robert M. Spann. 1971. "Supply Response in a Regulated Industry: The Case of Natural Gas." *Bell Journal of Economics and Management Science* 2, no. 1: 94–121.

Feezer, Lester W. 1938. "Manufacturer's Liability for Injuries Caused by His Products: Defective Automobiles." *Michigan Law Review* 37, no. 1: 1–27.

Feezer, Lester W. 1930. "Capacity to Bear Loss as a Factor in the Decision of Certain Types of Tort Cases." *University of Pennsylvania Law Review and American Law Register* 78, no. 7: 805–841.

Feezer, Lester W. 1931. "Capacity to Bear Loss as a Factor in the Decision of Certain Types of Tort Cases." *University of Pennsylvania Law Review* 79, no. 6: 742–767.

Feezer, Lester W., and Dwight Campbell, Jr. 1935. "Tort Liability of Manufacturers." *Minnesota Law Review* 19: 752–762.

Fisher, Franklin M., and Gerald Kraft. 1971. "The Effect of the Removal of the Firemen on Railroad Accidents, 1962–1967." *Bell Journal of Economics and Management Science* 2, no. 2: 470–494.

Friedmann, W.G. 1949. "Social Insurance and the Principles of Tort Liability." *Harvard Law Review* 63, no. 2: 241–265.

Furubotn, Eirik G., and Rudolf Richter. 1984. "The New Institutional Economics: Symposium June 6–10, 1983, Mettlach/Saar: Editorial Preface." *Journal of Institutional and Theoretical Economics/Zeitschrift für die gesamte Staatswissenschaft* 140, no. 1: 1–6.

Furubotn, Eirik G., and Rudolph Richter. 1993. "The New Institutional Economics: Bonded Rationality and the Analysis of State and Society." *Journal of Institutional and Theoretical Economics* 150, no. 1: 11–17.

Gerwig, Robert W. 1962. "Natural Gas Production: A Study of Costs of Regulation." *Journal of Law & Economics* 5: 69–92.

Goodhart, Arthur L. 1935. "Restatement of the Law of Torts, II." *University of Pennsylvania Law Review* 83: 968–996.

Green, Leon. 1928. "The Duty Problem in Negligence Cases." *Columbia Law Review* 28, no. 8 (December): 1014–1045.

Green, Leon. 1952–1953. "The Individual's Protection under Negligence Law: Risk Sharing." *Northwestern University Law Review* 47, no. 6: 751–777.

Greenberg, Edward. 1967. "Wire Television and the FCC's Second Report and Order on CATV Systems." *Journal of Law & Economics* 10: 181–192.

Gregory, Charles O. 1932. "Vicarious Responsibility and Contributory Negligence." *Yale Law Journal* 41, no. 6: 831–852.

Gregory, Charles O. 1938. "Contribution among Tortfeasors: A Uniform Practice." *Wisconsin Law Review* no. 3 (May): 365–401.

Gregory, Charles O. 1941. "Contribution among Joint Tortfeasors: A Defense." *Harvard Law Review* 54, no. 7: 1170–1177.

Hale, G.E., and Rosemary D. Hale. 1958. *Market Power: Size and Shape under the Sherman Act*. Boston: Little, Brown & Co.

Hale, Rosemary D. 1967. "Cookware: A Study in Vertical Integration." *Journal of Law & Economics* 10: 169–179.

Hale, Rosemary D., and G.E. Hale. 1962. "More on Mergers." *Journal of Law & Economics* 5: 119–130.

Harper, Fowler V. 1932. "Liability without Fault and Proximate Cause." *Michigan Law Review* 30, no. 7: 1001–1015.

Hartwell, Ronald Max. 1995. *A History of the Mont Pelerin Society*. Indianapolis: Liberty Fund.

Hilton, George W. 1966. "The Consistency of the Interstate Commerce Act." *Journal of Law & Economics* 9: 87–113.

Hirshleifer, Jack. 1959. "Capitalist Ethics–Tough or Soft?" *Journal of Law & Economics* 2 (October): 114–119.

Holmes, O.W., Jr. 1881. *The Common Law*. Boston: Little, Brown & Company.

James, Fleming, Jr. 1936. "Review of *Legislative Loss Distribution in Negligence Actions* by Charles O. Gregory." *University of Chicago Law Review* 4, no. 1: 158–162.

James, Fleming, Jr. 1938. "Last Clear Chance: A Transitional Doctrine." *Yale Law Journal* 47: 704–723.

James, Fleming, Jr. 1939. "Contribution among Tortfeasors in the Field of Accident Litigation." *Utah Bar Bulletin* 9 (December): 208–213.

James, Fleming, Jr. 1941. "Contribution Among Joint Tortfeasors: A Pragmatic Criticism." *Harvard Law Review* 54, no. 7: 1156–1169.

James, Fleming, Jr. 1946. "Accident Liability: Some Wartime Developments." *Yale Law Journal* 55, no. 2: 365–400.

James, Fleming, Jr. 1948. "Accident Liability Reconsidered: The Impact of Liability Insurance." *Yale Law Journal* 57, no. 4: 549–570.

James, Fleming, Jr. 1949. "Functions of Judge and Jury in Negligence Cases." *Yale Law Journal* 58, no. 5 (April): 667–690.

James, Fleming, Jr. 1950. "Chief Justice Maltbie and the Law of Negligence." *Connecticut Bar Journal* 24, no. 1 (March): 61–77.

James, Fleming, Jr. 1952. "Assumption of Risk." *Yale Law Journal* 61, no. 2 (February): 141–169.

James, Fleming, Jr. 1953. "Contributory Negligence." *Yale Law Journal* 62, no. 5 (April): 691–735.

James, Fleming, Jr., and John J. Dickinson. 1950. "Accident Proneness and Accident Law." *Harvard Law Review* 63, no. 5: 769–795.

James, Fleming, Jr., and Stuart C. Law. 1952. "Compensation for Auto Accident Victims: A Story of Too Little Too Late." *Connecticut Bar Journal* 26, no. 1 (March): 70–81.

James, Fleming, Jr., and John V. Thornton. 1950. "The Impact of Insurance on the Law of Torts." *Law and Contemporary Problems* 15, no. 3: 431–444.

Jeanblanc, Lindsey R. 1937. "Manufacturers' Liability to Persons Other than Their Immediate Vendees." *Virginia Law Review* 24, no. 2: 134–158.

Jewkes, John. 1953. "The Nationalization of Industry." *University of Chicago Law Review* 20, no. 4: 615–645.

Jewkes, John. 1958. "British Monopoly Policy 1944–56." *Journal of Law & Economics* 1 (October): 1–19.

Jewkes, John, David Sawers, and Richard Stillerman. 1958. *The Sources of Invention*. London: Macmillan and Co.; New York: St. Martin's Press.

Kahn, Alfred E. 1970–1971. *The Economics of Regulation: Principles and Institutions*. Hoboken, NJ: John Wiley & Sons.

Keeler, Theodore E. 1972. "Airline Regulation and Market Performance." *Bell Journal of Economics and Management Science* 3, no. 2: 399–424.

Kessel, Reuben A. 1967. "Economic Effects of Federal Regulation of Milk Markets." *Journal of Law & Economics* 10: 51–78.

Khazzoom, J. Daniel. 1971. "The FPC Staff's Econometric Model of Natural Gas Supply in the United States." *Bell Journal of Economics and Management Science* 2, no. 1: 51–93.

Kitch, Edmund W. 1968. "Regulation of the Field Market for Natural Gas by the Federal Power Commission." *Journal of Law & Economics* 11, no. 2: 243–280.

Kitch, Edmund W. 1972. "The Yellow Cab Antitrust Case." *Journal of Law & Economics* 15, no. 2: 327–336.

Kitch, Edmund W. 1983. "The Fire of Truth: A Remembrance of Law and Economics at Chicago, 1932–1970." *Journal of Law & Economics* 26, no. 1: 163–234.

Kitch, Edmund W., Marc Isaacson, and Daniel Kasper. 1971. "The Regulation of Taxicabs in Chicago." *Journal of Law & Economics* 14, no. 2: 285–350.

Knutson, Ronald D. 1969. "The Economic Consequences of the Minnesota Dairy Industry Unfair Trade Practices Act." *Journal of Law & Economics* 12, no. 2: 377–389.

Kronman, Anthony T. 1980. "Wealth Maximization as a Normative Principle." *Journal of Legal Studies* 9, no. 2: 227–242.

Lande, Robert H. 1989. "Wealth Transfers as the Primary Concern of the FTC Act." *Journal of Reprints for Antitrust Law and Economics* 19, no. 1: 159–184.

Landes, William M. 1971. "An Economic Analysis of the Courts." *Journal of Law and Economics* 14, no. 1 (April): 61–107.

Landes, William M., and Richard A. Posner. 1978. "Salvors, Finders, Good Samaritans, and Other Rescuers: An Economic Study of Law and Altruism." *Journal of Legal Studies* 7, no. 1: 83–128.

Landes, William M., and Richard A. Posner. 1980. "Joint and Multiple Tortfeasors: An Economic Analysis." *Journal of Legal Studies* 9, no. 3: 517–555.

Landes, William M., and Richard A. Posner. 1981. "An Economic Theory of Intentional Torts." *International Review of Law and Economics* 1, no. 2: 127–154.

Landes, William M., and Richard A. Posner. 1985. "A Positive Economic Analysis of Products Liability." *Journal of Legal Studies* 14, no. 3: 535–567.

Lees, D.S. 1962. "The Logic of the British National Health Service." *Journal of Law & Economics* 5 (October): 111–118.

Leff, Arthur Allen. 1974. "Economic Analysis of Law: Some Realism about Nominalism." *Virginia Law Review* 60, no. 3 (March): 451–482.

Leidy, Paul A. 1940. "Another New Tort?" *Michigan Law Review* 38, no. 7: 964–986.

Leidy, Paul A. 1942. "Tort Liability of Suppliers of Defective Chattels." *Michigan Law Review* 40, no. 5: 679–697.

Lerner, Abba P. 1964. "Conflicting Principles of Public Utility Price Regulation." *Journal of Law & Economics* 7: 61–70.

Letwin, William. 1965. *Law and Economic Policy in America: The Evolution of the Sherman Antitrust Act*. Chicago, IL and London: University of Chicago Press.

Levin, Harvey J. 1962. "Federal Control of Entry in the Broadcast Industry." *Journal of Law & Economics* 5: 49–67.

Levin, Harvey J. 1973. "Television's Second Chance: A Retrospective Look at the Sloan Cable Commission." *Bell Journal of Economics and Management Science* 4, no. 1: 343–365.

Levine, Michael E. 1969. "Landing Fees and the Airport Congestion Problem." *Journal of Law & Economics* 12, no. 1: 79–108.

Levine, Michael E. 1975. "Regulating Airmail Transportation." *Journal of Law & Economics* 18, no. 2: 317–359.

Levy, David M., and Sandra J. Peart. 2014. "Ronald Coase and the Fabian Society: Competitive Discussion in Liberal Ideology" (July 25). GMU Working Paper in Economics No. 14-29. Available at SSRN: https://ssrn.com/abstract=2472130 or http://dx.doi.org/10.2139/ssrn.2472130.

Lilly, Austin J. 1932. "Criticism of the Proposed Solution." *Columbia Law Review* 32, no. 5: 803–812.

Littlechild, S.C. 1970. "Peak-Load Pricing of Telephone Calls." *Bell Journal of Economics and Management Science* 1, no. 2: 191–210.

Litzenberger, Robert H., and Cherukuri U. Rao. 1971. "Estimates of the Marginal Rate of Time Preference and Average Risk Aversion of Investors in Electric Utility Shares: 1960–66." *Bell Journal of Economics and Management Science* 2, no. 1: 265–277.

Lurie, Melvin. 1960. "Government Regulation and Union Power: A Case Study of the Boston Transit Industry." *Journal of Law & Economics* 3 (October): 118–135.

MacAvoy, Paul W. 1965. *The Economic Effects of Regulation*. Cambridge, MA: MIT Press.

MacAvoy, Paul W. 1970. "The Effectiveness of the Federal Power Commission." *Bell Journal of Economics and Management Science* 1, no. 2: 271–303.

MacAvoy, Paul W. 1971a. "The Regulation-Induced Shortage of Natural Gas." *Journal of Law & Economics* 14, no. 1: 167–199.

MacAvoy, Paul W. 1971b. "The Formal Work-Product of the Federal Power Commissioners." *Bell Journal of Economics and Management Science* 2, no. 1: 379–395.

MacAvoy, Paul W., and Robert S. Pindyck. 1973. "Alternative Regulatory Policies for Dealing with the Natural Gas Shortage." *Bell Journal of Economics and Management Science* 4, no. 2: 454–498.

MacIntyre, Malcolm M. 1940. "The Rationale of Last Clear Chance." *Harvard Law Review* 53, no. 8: 1225–1252.

Mann, Patrick C. 1974. "User Power and Electricity Rates." *Journal of Law & Economics* 17, no. 2: 433–443.

Manne, Henry G. 1962. "The 'Higher Criticism' of the Modern Corporation." *Columbia Law Review* 62, no. 3: 399–432.

Manne, Henry G. 1964. "Some Theoretical Aspects of Share Voting. An Essay in Honor of Adolf A. Berle." *Columbia Law Review* 64, no. 8: 1427–1445.

Manne, Henry G. 1965. "Mergers and the Market for Corporate Control." *Journal of Political Economy* 73, no. 2: 110–120.

Manne, Henry G. 1966a. *Insider Trading and the Stock Market.* New York: Free Press.

Manne, Henry G. 1966b. "In Defense of Insider Trading." *Harvard Business Review* 44: 113–122.

Manne, Henry G. 1967a. "Insider Trading and the Administrative Process." *George Washington Law Review* 35, no. 3 (March): 473–511.

Manne, Henry G. 1967b. "Cash Tender Offers for Shares: A Reply to Chairman Cohen." *Duke Law Journal* 1967, no. 2: 231–253.

Manne, Henry G. 1967c. "Our Two Corporation Systems: Law and Economics." *Virginia Law Review* 53, no. 2: 259–284.

McCraw, Thomas K. 1984. *Prophets of Regulation: Charles Francis Adams, Louis D. Brandeis, James M. Landis, Alfred E. Kahn.* Cambridge, MA: Harvard University Press.

McGee, John S. 1956. "Price Discrimination and Competitive Effects: The Standard Oil of Indiana Case." *University of Chicago Law Review* 23, no. 3: 398–473.

McGee, John S. 1958. "Predatory Price Cutting: The Standard Oil (N. J.) Case." *Journal of Law & Economics* 1 (October): 137–169.

McGee, John S. 1960. "Ocean Freight Rate Conferences and the American Merchant Marine." *University of Chicago Law Review* 27, no. 2: 191–314.

McGee, John S. 1964. "Government Intervention in the Spanish Sugar Industry." *Journal of Law & Economics* 7: 121–172.

McGee, John S. 1966. "Patent Exploitation: Some Economic and Legal Problems." *Journal of Law and Economics* 9: 135–162.

McNiece, Harold F., and John V. Thornton. 1949. "Affirmative Duties in Tort." *Yale Law Journal* 58, no. 8: 1272–1289.

Mechem, Floyd R. 1910. "Employers' Liability." *American Law Review* 44, no. 2 (March–April): 221–255.

Mentschikoff, Soia. 1952. "The Significance of Arbitration: A Preliminary Inquiry." *Law and Contemporary Problems* 17 (Fall): 698–710.

Michelman, Frank. 1979. "A Comment on 'Some Uses and Abuses of Economics in Law.'" *University of Chicago Law Review* 46: 307–315.

Minasian, Jora R. 1964. "Television Pricing and the Theory of Public Goods." *Journal of Law & Economics* 7: 71–80.

Moore, Thomas G. 1961. "The Purpose of Licensing." *Journal of Law & Economics* 4 (October): 93–117.

Morris, Clarence. 1952. "Hazardous Enterprises and Risk Bearing Capacity." *Yale Law Journal* 61, no. 7: 1172–1179.

Nelson, James R. 1971. "The Ralph Nader Study Group Report on the Interstate Commerce Commission." *Bell Journal of Economics and Management Science* 2, no. 1: 330–336.

New York Law Revision Commission. 1943. *Recommendation Relating to Warranties of Fitness in Report of the Law Revision Committee for 1943*: 413.

Nixon, Richard M. 1936. "Changing Rules of Liability in Automobile Accident Litigation." *Law and Contemporary Problems* 3, no. 4: 476–490.

Ohls, James C. 1970. "Marginal Cost Pricing, Investment Theory and CATV: A Reply." *Journal of Law & Economics* 14, no. 2: 517–519.

Palmer, John. 1973. "A Further Analysis of Provincial Trucking Regulation." *Bell Journal of Economics and Management Science* 4, no. 2: 655–664.

Park, Rolla Edward. 1972. "Prospects for Cable in the 100 Largest Television Markets." *Bell Journal of Economics and Management Science* 3, no. 1: 130–150.

Peltzman, Sam. 1971. "Pricing in Public and Private Enterprises: Electric Utilities in the United States." *Journal of Law & Economics* 14, no. 1: 109–147.

Peterman, John L. 1965. "The Structure of National Time Rates in the Television Broadcasting Industry." *Journal of Law & Economics* 8 (October): 77–131.

Peterman, John L. 1975a. "The Brown Shoe Case." *Journal of Law & Economics* 18, no. 1: 81–146.

Peterman, John L. 1975b. "The Federal Trade Commission V. Brown Shoe Company." *Journal of Law & Economics* 18, no. 2: 361–419.

Peterman, John L. 1979. "The International Salt Case." *Journal of Law & Economics* 22, no. 2: 351–364.

Plott, Charles R. 1965. "Occupational Self-Regulation: A Case Study of the Oklahoma Dry Cleaners." *Journal of Law & Economics* 8: 195–222.

Posner, Richard A. 1968a. "Natural Monopoly and Its Regulation." *Stanford Law Review* 21: 548–643.

Posner, Richard A. 1968b. "Oligopoly and the Antitrust Laws: A Suggested Approach." *Stanford Law Review* 21: 1562–1606.

Posner, Richard A. 1970. "Review of *The Costs of Accidents: A Legal and Economic Analysis* by Guido Calabresi." *University of Chicago Law Review* 37, no. 3: 636–648.

Posner, Richard A. 1971a. "Killing or Wounding to Protect a Property Interest." *Journal of Law & Economics* 14, no. 1: 201–232.

Posner, Richard A. 1971b. "Taxation by Regulation." *Bell Journal of Economics and Management Science* 2, no. 1: 22–50.

Posner, Richard A. 1972a. "The Appropriate Scope of Regulation in the Cable Television Industry." *Bell Journal of Economics and Management Science* 3, no. 1: 98–129.

Posner, Richard A. 1972b. "A Theory of Negligence." *Journal of Legal Studies* 1, no. 1: 29–96.

Posner, Richard A. 1973a. "An Economic Approach to Legal Procedure and Judicial Administration." *Journal of Legal Studies* 2, no. 2 (June): 399–458.

Posner, Richard A. 1973b. *Economic Analysis of Law*. Boston, MA: Little, Brown & Company.

Posner, Richard A. 1975. "The Economic Approach to Law." *Texas Law Review* 53, no. 4 (May): 757–782.

Posner, Richard A. 1977. "Gratuitous Promises in Economics and Law." *Journal of Legal Studies* 6, no. 2: 411–426.

Posner, Richard A. 1978. "The Right of Privacy." *Georgia Law Review* 12 (Spring): 393–422.

Posner, Richard A. 1979. "Utilitarianism, Economics, and Legal Theory." *Journal of Legal Studies* 8, no. 1: 103–140.

Posner, Richard A. 1980a. "The Ethical and Political Basis of the Efficiency Norm in Common Law Adjudication." *Hofstra Law Review* 8, no. 3 (Spring): 487–508.

Posner, Richard A. 1980b. "The Value of Wealth: A Comment on Dworkin and Kronman." *Journal of Legal Studies* 9, no. 2: 243–252.

Posner, Richard A. 1981. *The Economics of Justice*. Cambridge, MA: Harvard University Press.

Posner, Richard A. 1985. "An Economic Theory of the Criminal Law." *Columbia Law Review* 85, no. 6: 1193–1231.

Posner, Richard A. 1992. *Sex and Reason*. Cambridge, MA: Harvard University Press.

Posner, Richard A. 1993a. "The New Institutional Economics Meets Law and Economics." *Journal of Institutional and Theoretical Economics (JITE)/Zeitschrift für die gesamte Staatswissenschaft* 149, no. 1: 73–87.

Posner, Richard A. 1993b. "Nobel Laureate: Ronald Coase and Methodology." *Journal of Economic Perspectives* 7, no. 4: 195–210.

Posner, Richard A. 1995. *Aging and Old Age*. Chicago, IL and London: University of Chicago Press.

Posner, Richard A. 2005a. *Preventing Surprise Attacks: Intelligence Reform in the Wake of 9/11*. Stanford, CA: Roman & Littlefield.

Posner, Richard A. 2005b. *Remaking Domestic Intelligence*. Stanford, CA: Hoover Institution Press.

Posner, Richard A. 2006a. *Not a Suicide Pact: The Constitution in a Time of National Emergency*. New York: Oxford University Press.

Posner, Richard A. 2006b. *Uncertain Shield: The U.S. Intelligence System in the Throes of Reform*. Lanham, MD: Rowman & Littlefield/Hoover Institution Press.

Posner, Richard A. 2007. *Countering Terrorism: Blurred Focus, Halting Steps*. Lanham, MD: Rowman & Littlefield.

Posner, Richard A. 2008. *A Failure of Capitalism: The Crisis of '08 and the Descent into Depression*. Cambridge, MA: Harvard University Press.

Posner, Richard A. 2014. *Economic Analysis of Law*. 9th ed. New York: Wolters Kluwer Law & Business.

Posner, Richard A., and William M. Landes. 1980. "The Positive Economic Theory of Tort Law." *Georgia Law Review* 5: 851–924.

Posner, Richard A., and Andrew M. Rosenfield. 1977. "Impossibility and Related Doctrines in Contract Law: An Economic Analysis." *Journal of Legal Studies* 6, no. 1: 83–118.

Priest, George L. 1975. "The History of the Postal Monopoly in the United States." *Journal of Law & Economics* 18, no. 1: 33–80.

Priest, George L. 1983. "Social Science Theory and Legal Education: The Law School as University." *Journal of Legal Education* 33, no. 3: 437–441.

Priest, George L. 1985. "The Invention of Enterprise Liability: A Critical History of the Intellectual Foundations of Modern Tort Law." *Journal of Legal Studies* 14, no. 3: 461–527.

Priest, George L. 1987. "The Current Insurance Crisis and Modern Tort Law." *Yale Law Journal* 96, no. 7: 1521–1590.

Priest, George L. 1999. "Henry Manne and the Market Measure of Intellectual Influence." *Case Western Reserve Law Review* 50, no. 2 (Winter): 325–332.

Priest, George L. 2005. "The Rise of Law and Economics: A Memoir of the Early Years." In *Law and Economics: Essays by the Founding Fathers*, eds. Charles K. Rowley and Francesco Parisi, 350–382. Cheltenham: Edward Elgar.

Priest, George L. 2008. "The Abiding Influence of the Antitrust Paradox: An Essay in Honor of Robert H. Bork." *Harvard Journal of Law & Public Policy* 31, no. 2 (Spring): 455–466.

Priest, George L. 2010. "The Limits of Antitrust and the Chicago School Tradition." *Journal of Competition Law and Economics* 6, no. 1: 1–9.

Priest, George L. 2012. "Rethinking the Economic Basis of the Standard Oil Refining Monopoly: Dominance against Competing Cartels." *Southern California Law Review* 85, no. 1: 499–558.

Priest, George L. 2014a. "Ronald Coase: Firms and Markets." *Man and the Economy* 1, no. 2: 143–157.

Priest, George L. 2014b. "Bork's Strategy and the Influence of the Chicago School on Modern Antitrust Law." *Journal of Law & Economics* 57, no. S3: S1–S17.

Priest, George L. 2017. "A Principled Approach toward Insurance Law: The Economics of Insurance and the Current Restatement Project." *George Mason Law Review* 24, no. 3 (Spring): 635–662.

Priest, George L., and Benjamin Klein. 1984. "The Selection of Disputes for Litigation." *Journal of Legal Studies* 13, no. 1 (January): 1–55.

Priest, George L., and William Ranney Levi. 2010. "Stevens and Antitrust." *National Law Journal (Online)*, May 24. Archived.

Priest, George L., and Jonathan Lewinsohn. 2007. "Aspen Skiing: Product Differentiation and Preventing Free Riding as Monopolization." In *Antitrust Stories*, eds. Eleanor M. Fox and Daniel A. Crane, 229–255. New York: Foundation Press.

Prosser, William L. 1941. *Handbook of the Law of Torts*. St. Paul, MN: West Publishing Co.

Prosser, William L. 1943. "The Implied Warranty of Merchantable Quality." *Minnesota Law Review* 27, no. 2 (January): 117–168.

Prosser, William L. 1948. "Contributory Negligence as Defense to Violation of Statute." *Minnesota Law Review* 32, no. 2 (January): 105–128.

Reder, Melvin W. 1982. "Chicago Economics: Permanence and Change." *Journal of Economic Literature* 20, no. 1: 1–38.

Rees, Albert. 1959. "Do Unions Cause Inflation?" *Journal of Law & Economics* 2: 84–94.

Rubin, Paul H. 1999. "Henry G. Manne, Network Entrepreneur." *Case Western Reserve Law Review* 50, no. 2: 333–339.

Russell, A.J. 1933. "Manufacturers' Liability to the Ultimate Consumer." *Kentucky Law Journal* 21, no. 4 (May): 388–406.

Sabel, Stanley Law. 1938. "The Uncompensated Industrial Injury." *Michigan Law Review* 36, no. 6: 935–961.

Schwartz, Warren F. 1999. "What Do I Do for the Economists?" *Case Western Law Review* 50: 347–350.

Scott, Kenneth E. 1993. "The New Institutional Economics Meets Law and Economics: Comment." *Journal of Institutional and Theoretical Economics (Jite)/Zeitschrift für die gesamte Staatswissenschaft* 149, no. 1: 92–95.

Seavey, Warren A. 1939. "Mr. Justice Cardozo and the Law of Torts." *Yale Law Journal* 48, no. 3: 390–425.

Secretary. 1959. "The Sumptuary Manifesto." *Journal of Law & Economics* 2 (October): 120–123.

Shavell, Steven. 1980. "Strict Liability versus Negligence." *Journal of Legal Studies* 9, no. 1: 1–25.

Siegan, Bernard H. 1970. "Non-Zoning in Houston." *Journal of Law & Economics* 13, no. 1: 71–147.

Sloss, James. 1970. "Regulation of Motor Freight Transportation: A Quantitative Evaluation of Policy." *Bell Journal of Economics and Management Science* 1, no. 2: 327–366.

Smith, Jeremiah. 1914a. "Sequel to Workmen's Compensation Acts." *Harvard Law Review* 27, no. 3: 235–259.

Smith, Jeremiah. 1914b. "Sequel to Workmen's Compensation Acts." *Harvard Law Review* 27, no. 4: 344–368.

Smith, Young B. 1923. "Frolic and Detour." *Columbia Law Review* 23, no. 5: 444–463.

Smith, Young B. 1932. "The Problem and Its Solution." *Columbia Law Review* 32, no. 5: 785–803.

Spann, Robert M., and Edward W. Erickson. 1970. "The Economics of Railroading: The Beginning of Cartelization and Regulation." *Bell Journal of Economics and Management Science* 1, no. 2: 227–244.

Squire, Lyn. 1973. "Some Aspects of Optimal Pricing for Telecommunications." *Bell Journal of Economics and Management Science* 4, no. 2: 515–525.

Steele, Henry. 1962. "Monopoly and Competition in the Ethical Drugs Market." *Journal of Law & Economics* 5 (October): 131–163.

Stigler, George J. 1961. "Private Vice and Public Virtue." *Journal of Law & Economics* 4: 1–11.

Stigler, George J. 1964. "A Theory of Oligopoly." *Journal of Political Economy* 72, no. 1: 44–61.

Stigler, George J. 1965. "The Dominant Firm and the Inverted Umbrella." *Journal of Law & Economics* 8 (October): 167–172.

Stigler, George J. 1971. "The Theory of Economic Regulation." *Bell Journal of Economics and Management Science* 2, no. 1: 3–21.

Stigler, George J., and Claire Friedland. 1962. "What Can Regulators Regulate? The Case of Electricity." *Journal of Law & Economics* 5: 1–16.

Stone, Christopher D. 1963. "Closed Territorial Distribution: An Opening Question in the Sherman Act." *University of Chicago Law Review* 30, no. 2: 286–317.

Stroup, Richard, and John Baden. 1973. "Externality, Property Rights, and the Management of Our National Forests." *Journal of Law & Economics* 16, no. 2: 303–312.

Stull, William J. 1975. "Community Environment, Zoning, and the Market Value of Single-Family Homes." *Journal of Law & Economics* 18, no. 2: 535–557.

Teles, Steven M. 2008. *The Rise of the Conservative Legal Movement.* Princeton, NJ: Princeton University Press.

Telser, Lester G. 1960. "Why Should Manufacturers Want Fair Trade?" *Journal of Law & Economics* 3 (October): 86–105.

Terry, Henry T. 1915. "Negligence." *Harvard Law Review* 29, no. 1 (November): 40–54.

Thayer, Ezra Ripley. 1916. "Liability without Fault." *Harvard Law Review* 29, no. 8: 801–896.

Thompson, Howard E., and George C. Tiao. 1971. "Analysis of Telephone Data: A Case Study of Forecasting Seasonal Time Series." *Bell Journal of Economics and Management Science* 2, no. 2: 515–541.

Tribe, Keith. 2009. "Liberalism and Neoliberalism in Britain, 1930–1980." In *The Road from Mont Pelerin: The Making of the Neoliberal Thought Collective*, ed. Philip Mirowski and Dieter Plehwe, 68–97. Cambridge, MA: Harvard University Press.

Tullock, Gordon. 1974. "Review of *Economic Analysis of Law* by Richard A. Posner." *Public Choice* 17: 122–123.

Urban, Raymond, and Richard Mancke. 1972. "Federal Regulation of Whiskey Labelling: From the Repeal of Prohibition to the Present." *Journal of Law & Economics* 15, no. 2: 411–426.

Van Doren, Peter, and Thomas A. Firey. 2017. "Regulation at 40." *Regulation* 40, no. 1 (Spring): 30–37.

Verleger, Philip. 1973. "Review of George C. Eads' *The Local Service Air Line Experiment*." *Bell Journal of Economics and Management Science* 4, no. 2: 682–684.

Viner, Jacob. 1960. "The Intellectual History of Laissez Faire." *Journal of Law and Economics* 3 (October): 45–69.

Wechsler, Herbert. 1959. "Toward Neutral Principles of Constitutional Law." *Harvard Law Review* 73, no. 1 (November): 1–35.

Weinrib, Ernest J. 1980. "Utilitarianism, Economics, and Legal Theory." *University of Toronto Law Journal* 30, no. 3: 307–332.

Weiss, Roger W. 1964. "The Case for Federal Meat Inspection Examined." *Journal of Law & Economics* 7: 107–120.

White, G. Edward. 1980. *Tort Law in America: An Intellectual History*. New York: Oxford University Press.

Whitehurst, Clinton H. 1965. "The Merchant Marine Act of 1936: An Operational Subsidy in Retrospect." *Journal of Law & Economics* 8: 223–242.

Williamson, Oliver E. 1993. "The Evolving Science of Organization." *Journal of Institutional and Theoretical Economics (Jite)/Zeitschrift für die gesamte Staatswissenschaft* 149, no. 1: 36–63.

Winfield, Percy H. 1934. "Duty in Tortious Negligence." *Columbia Law Review* 34, no. 1: 41–66.

INDEX